WITHDRAWN FROM LIBRARY

W9-CHA-847

Great Jobs

for

Economics
Majors

MONTGOMERY COLLEGE
ROCKVILLE CAMPUS LIBRARY
ROCKVILLE, MARYLAND

Great Jobs

for

Economics Majors

Blythe Camenson

SERIES DEVELOPERS AND CONTRIBUTING AUTHORS
Stephen Lambert
Julie DeGalan

VGM Career Horizons
NTC/Contemporary Publishing Group

272593 OCT 0 9 2002

Library of Congress Cataloging-in-Publication Data

Camenson, Blythe.
    Great jobs for economics majors / Blythe Camenson.
        p.   cm.
    Includes index.
    ISBN 0-658-00222-8
    1. Vocational guidance—United States.   I. Title.
  HF5382.5.U5C25196   2000
  330′.023′73—dc21   99-44167
                                      CIP

Published by VGM Career Horizons
A division of NTC/Contemporary Publishing Group, Inc.
4255 West Touhy Avenue, Lincolnwood (Chicago), Illinois 60712-1975 U.S.A.
Copyright © 2000 by NTC/Contemporary Publishing Group, Inc.
All rights reserved. No part of this book may be reproduced, stored in a retrieval
system, or transmitted in any form or by any means, electronic, mechanical,
photocopying, recording, or otherwise, without the prior written permission of
NTC/Contemporary Publishing Group, Inc.
Printed in the United States of America
International Standard Book Number: 0-658-00222-8

00   01   02   03   04   05   LB   15   14   13   12   11   10   9   8   7   6   5   2   1

CONTENTS

Acknowledgments

The author would like to thank the following professionals for providing information and advice on careers for economics majors:

Robyn Bramhall, human resources

Chris Fuller, marketing and sales

J. Douglas Nobles, loan officer

Jim Van Laningham, U.S. Foreign Service

ECONOMICS: PLOTTING YOUR FUTURE

"Economics is the art of trying to satisfy infinite needs with limited resources."

—Albert Camus

You've heard this before (most likely from engineering majors or students in some other techie field): "Oh, economics. You'll be able to understand the *Wall Street Journal*, but what kind of job do you think you'll get?"

Or maybe this even more negative statement: "There's absolutely nothing you can do with a bachelor's in economics."

As many students do, you might be progressing through your economics program, semester after semester, year after year, taking your major courses and signing up for electives but not really sure where you'll be on graduation day, never mind five or ten years from now.

Maybe some not so savvy friends or family members have given you the following advice: "If you want to have a career, you need to be in some sort of professional program. Nursing. Business. Engineering. Agriculture. Accounting. Anything but economics."

And, in your gut, you worry they're right. But those professional programs aren't for you. The fields don't interest you.

So, what in the world *are* you going to do with that B.A. or B.S. in economics? Have you been on a dead-end path? Will you graduate with nothing more than the ability to entertain guests at a cocktail party with conversation on Dow Jones averages or the latest trends revealed in *Consumer Reports*? And how will you be able to give that party without an income? There is one thing you know for sure: intelligent conversation does not pay the bills.

Now is the time to put all those fears aside. With some advance planning and an acquired understanding of your options, you will find that your career choices are as diverse as the number of economics majors. Even more so.

It is true that a bachelor's degree in any field is no guarantee of a job these days, unless you are in a technical field, such as computers and some natural sciences. However, walking into a job with a bachelor's degree might not be as impossible as you—or your friends and family—think. You just have to be creative and imaginative.

Economics is a broad field, so employment possibilities are similarly broad. As with other fields, the more education, training, and experience you have, the better your chances of employment. Those with the best college records and a willingness to relocate have the best chances to find the job of their choice.

WHAT IS ECONOMICS?

Economics is the study of the way society uses its limited resources to produce the goods and services that it needs. It is a social science that studies many of the problems facing our society, and it is the foundation of most theories of business finance, management, and marketing.

Economics provides a logical, ordered way of looking at various problems. Whether we are discussing how a firm decides where to locate a business, how individuals choose where to invest their money, or how the federal government determines how to balance the budget, each is faced with the problem of making a decision about the best use of limited resources. Economics provides a logical method of analyzing the trade-offs involved in the decision-making process.

ECONOMICS SPECIALIZATIONS

There are many fields within economics. Microeconomics is the study of smaller units of the economy, such as firms and households, and is often concerned with issues like competition, markets, prices, incomes, and efficiency. Macroeconomics is the study of the aggregate economy. It focuses on inflation, unemployment, interest rates, economic growth, taxation, international trade, and international financial flows. Other areas of economics specialization include labor issues, urban topics, international economics, economic development, comparative economic systems, money and banking, health care, public finance, law and economics, transportation, the gaming industry, natural resource economics, common markets, econometrics, and mathematical economics.

THE SKILLS YOU'LL ACQUIRE

Economics is a powerful tool that helps you understand the world better. It is the foundation of all business studies. Economics majors have a good deal of institutional knowledge about the business world, the economic environment in which businesses operate, and the government policies that affect businesses. Further, economics majors are viewed as having developed their ability to analyze and communicate the results of their analysis.

A major in economics is attractive to job recruiters and graduate school admissions directors because of the excellent background it provides in critical thinking and quantitative analysis.

WHAT CAN YOU DO WITH A MAJOR IN ECONOMICS?

Jobs held by economists are spread throughout many occupations. A major in economics prepares you for a wide range of professional careers.

Managerial training programs in many firms, including banks, other financial institutions, and large manufacturing companies, are open to economics majors. Economists are employed by businesses to study market problems, make predictions concerning market trends, and analyze how the overall economic system will affect a particular industry.

There are many opportunities for economics-related employment in government at the local, state, and federal levels. Economists working in government analyze public policy issues such as taxation, labor markets, welfare, international trade, and transportation.

Research and consulting firms also employ economists in such areas as forecasting and industry analysis.

Academic economists teach and do research on a variety of theoretical and applied topics.

An undergraduate degree in economics provides excellent preparation for graduate programs in law, business, and social sciences including economics.

In Chapters 9 through 14, you'll learn more details about these and many other career paths.

PART ONE

THE JOB SEARCH

CHAPTER ONE

THE SELF-ASSESSMENT

Self-assessment is the process by which you begin to acknowledge your own particular blend of education, experiences, values, needs, and goals. It provides the foundation for career planning and the entire job search process. Self-assessment involves looking inward and asking yourself what can sometimes prove to be difficult questions. This self-examination should lead to an intimate understanding of your personal traits, your personal values, your consumption patterns and economic needs, your longer-term goals, your skill base, your preferred skills, and your under-developed skills.

You come to the self-assessment process knowing yourself well in some of these areas, but you may still be uncertain about other aspects. You may be well aware of your consumption patterns, but have you spent much time specifically identifying your longer-term goals or your personal values as they relate to work? No matter what level of self-assessment you have undertaken to date, it is now time to clarify all of these issues and questions as they relate to the job search.

The knowledge you gain in the self-assessment process will guide the rest of your job search. In this book, you will learn about all of the following tasks:

- Writing resumes
- Exploring possible job titles
- Identifying employment sites
- Networking
- Interviewing
- Following up
- Evaluating job offers

In each of these steps, you will rely on and return often to the understanding gained through your self-assessment. Any individual seeking employment must be able and willing to express these facets of his or her personality to recruiters and interviewers throughout the job search. This communication allows you to show the world who you are so that together with employers you can determine whether there will be a workable match with a given job or career path.

HOW TO CONDUCT A SELF-ASSESSMENT

The self-assessment process goes on naturally all the time. People ask you to clarify what you mean, or you make a purchasing decision, or you begin a new relationship. You react to the world and the world reacts to you. How you understand these interactions and any changes you might make because of them are part of the natural process of self-discovery. There is, however, a more comprehensive and efficient way to approach self-assessment with regard to employment.

Because self-assessment can become a complex exercise, we have distilled it into a seven-step process that provides an effective basis for undertaking a job search. The seven steps include the following:

1. Understanding your personal traits

2. Identifying your personal values

3. Calculating your economic needs

4. Exploring your longer-term goals

5. Enumerating your skill base

6. Recognizing your preferred skills

7. Assessing skills needing further development

As you work through your self-assessment, you might want to create a worksheet similar to the one shown in Exhibit 1.1. Or you might want to keep a journal of the thoughts you have as you undergo this process. There will be many opportunities to revise your self-assessment as you start down the path of seeking a career.

STEP 1: Understanding Your Personal Traits
Each person has a unique personality that he or she brings to the job search process. Gaining a better understanding of your personal traits can help you

---

Exhibit 1.1

Self-Assessment Worksheet

STEP 1: Understand Your Personal Traits
The personal traits that describe me are:
(Include all of the words that describe you.)

The ten personal traits that most accurately describe me are: *(List these ten traits.)*

STEP 2: Identify Your Personal Values
Working conditions that are important to me include:
(List working conditions that would have to exist for you to accept a position.)

The values that go along with my working conditions are:
(Write down the values that correspond to each working condition.)

Some additional values I've decided to include are:
(List those values you identify as you conduct this job search.)

STEP 3: Calculate Your Economic Needs
My estimated minimum annual salary requirement is:
(Write the salary you have calculated based on your budget.)

Starting salaries for the positions I'm considering are:
(List the name of each job you are considering and the associated starting salary.)

STEP 4: Explore Your Longer-Term Goals
My thoughts on longer-term goals right now are:
(Jot down some of your longer-term goals as you know them right now.)

STEP 5: Enumerate Your Skill Base
The general skills I possess are: *(List the skills that underlie tasks you are able to complete.)*

The specific skills I possess are:
(List more technical or specific skills that you possess and indicate your level of expertise.)

General and specific skills that I want to promote to employers for the jobs I'm considering are:
(List general and specific skills for each type of job you are considering.)

STEP 6: Recognize Your Preferred Skills
Skills that I would like to use on the job include:
(List skills that you hope to use on the job, and indicate how often you'd like to use them.)

STEP 7: Assess Skills Needing Further Development
Some skills that I'll need to acquire for the jobs I'm considering include:
(Write down skills listed in job advertisements or job descriptions that you don't currently possess.)

I believe I can build these skills by:
(Describe how you plan to acquire these skills.)

evaluate job and career choices. Identifying these traits, and then finding employment that allows you to draw on at least some of them, can create a rewarding and fulfilling work experience. If potential employment doesn't allow you to use these preferred traits, it is important to decide whether you can find other ways to express them or whether you would be better off not considering this type of job. Interests and hobbies pursued outside of work hours can be one way to use personal traits you don't have an opportunity to draw on in your work. For example, if you consider yourself an outgoing person and the kinds of jobs you are examining allow little contact with other people, you may be able to achieve the level of interaction that is comfortable for you outside of your work setting. If such a compromise seems impractical or otherwise unsatisfactory, you probably should explore only jobs that provide the interaction you want and need on the job.

Many young adults who are not very confident about their attractiveness to employers will downplay their need for income. They will say, "Money is not all that important if I love my work." But if you begin to document exactly what you need for housing, transportation, insurance, clothing, food, and utilities, you will begin to understand that some jobs cannot meet your financial needs no matter how wonderful they are. If you have to worry each payday about bills and other financial obligations, you won't be very effective on the job. Begin now to be honest with yourself about your needs.

Inventorying Your Personal Traits. Begin the self-assessment process by creating an inventory of your personal traits. Using the list in Exhibit 1.2, decide which personal traits describe you.

Exhibit 1.2

Personal Traits

Accurate	Considerate	Fair-minded
Active	Cool	Farsighted
Adaptable	Cooperative	Feeling
Adventurous	Courageous	Firm
Affectionate	Critical	Flexible
Aggressive	Curious	Formal
Ambitious	Daring	Friendly
Analytical	Decisive	Future-oriented
Appreciative	Deliberate	Generous
Artistic	Detail-oriented	Gentle
Brave	Determined	Good-natured
Businesslike	Discreet	Helpful
Calm	Dominant	Honest
Capable	Eager	Humorous
Caring	Easygoing	Idealistic
Cautious	Efficient	Imaginative
Cheerful	Emotional	Impersonal
Clean	Empathetic	Independent
Competent	Energetic	Individualistic
Confident	Excitable	Industrious
Conscientious	Expressive	Informal
Conservative	Extroverted	Innovative

Intellectual	Peaceable	Self-disciplined
Intelligent	Personable	Sensible
Introverted	Persuasive	Sensitive
Intuitive	Pleasant	Serious
Inventive	Poised	Sincere
Jovial	Polite	Sociable
Just	Practical	Spontaneous
Kind	Precise	Strong
Liberal	Principled	Strong-minded
Likable	Private	Structured
Logical	Productive	Subjective
Loyal	Progressive	Tactful
Mature	Quick	Thorough
Methodical	Quiet	Thoughtful
Meticulous	Rational	Tolerant
Mistrustful	Realistic	Trusting
Modest	Receptive	Trustworthy
Motivated	Reflective	Truthful
Objective	Relaxed	Understanding
Observant	Reliable	Unexcitable
Open-minded	Reserved	Uninhibited
Opportunistic	Resourceful	Verbal
Optimistic	Responsible	Versatile
Organized	Reverent	Wholesome
Original	Sedentary	Wise
Outgoing	Self-confident	
Patient	Self-controlled	

Focusing on Selected Personal Traits. Of all the traits you identified from the list in Exhibit 1.2, select the ten you believe most accurately describe you. If you are having a difficult time deciding, think about which words people who know you well would use to describe you. Keep track of these ten traits.

Considering Your Personal Traits in the Job Search Process. As you begin exploring jobs and careers, watch for matches between your personal traits and the job descriptions you read. Some jobs will require many personal traits you know you possess, and others will not seem to match those traits.

· ·

A research assistant's work, for example, requires self-discipline, motivation, curiosity, and observation.

> Researchers often work alone, with limited opportunities to interact with others. Professors, on the other hand, must interact regularly with students and colleagues to carry out the teaching program. Educators need strong interpersonal and verbal skills, imagination, and a good sense of humor. They must enjoy being in front of groups and must become skilled at presenting information using a variety of methods.

Your decision-making ability, productivity, creativity, and verbal skills all have a bearing on your success in and enjoyment of your work life. To better guarantee success, be sure to take the time needed to understand these traits in yourself.

STEP 2: Identifying Your Personal Values

Your personal values affect every aspect of your life, including employment, and they develop and change as you move through life. Values can be defined as principles that we hold in high regard, qualities that are important and desirable to us. Some values aren't ordinarily connected to work (love, beauty, color, light, marriage, family, or religion), and others are (autonomy, cooperation, effectiveness, achievement, knowledge, and security). Our values determine, in part, the level of satisfaction we feel in a particular job.

Defining Acceptable Working Conditions. One facet of employment is the set of working conditions that must exist for someone to consider taking a job. Each of us would probably create a unique list of acceptable working conditions, but items that might be included on many people's lists are the amount of money you would need to be paid, how far you are willing to drive or travel, the amount of freedom you want in determining your own schedule, whether you would be working with people or data or things, and the types of tasks you would be willing to do. Your conditions might include statements of working conditions you will *not* accept; for example, you might not be willing to work at night or on weekends or holidays.

If you were offered a job tomorrow, what conditions would have to exist for you to realistically consider accepting the position? Take some time to make a list of these conditions.

Realizing Associated Values. Your list of working conditions can be used to create an inventory of your values relating to jobs and careers you are explor-

Exhibit 1.3

Work Values

Achievement	Development	Physical activity
Advancement	Effectiveness	Power
Adventure	Excitement	Precision
Attainment	Fast pace	Prestige
Authority	Financial gain	Privacy
Autonomy	Helping	Profit
Belonging	Humor	Recognition
Challenge	Improvisation	Risk
Change	Independence	Security
Communication	Influencing others	Self-expression
Community	Intellectual stimulation	Solitude
Competition	Interaction	Stability
Completion	Knowledge	Status
Contribution	Leading	Structure
Control	Mastery	Supervision
Cooperation	Mobility	Surroundings
Creativity	Moral fulfillment	Time freedom
Decision making	Organization	Variety

ing. For example, if one of your conditions stated that you wanted to earn at least $25,000 per year, the associated value would be financial gain. If another condition is to work with a friendly group of people, the value that goes along with that might be belonging or interaction with people. Exhibit 1.3 provides a list of commonly held values that relate to the work environment; use it to create your own list of personal values.

Relating Your Values to the World of Work. As you read the job descriptions in this book and in other suggested resources, think about the values associated with each position.

••

> For example, a financial adviser in an investment firm might be responsible for researching various investments, communicating the results of the research to clients, and arranging for the purchase of funds, stocks, or bonds. Some of the associated values are achievement, profit, and effectiveness.

••

If you were thinking about a career in this field, or any other field you're exploring, at least some of the associated values should match those you extracted from your list of working conditions. Take a second look at any values that don't match up. How important are they to you? What will happen if they are not satisfied on the job? Can you incorporate those personal values elsewhere? Your answers need to be brutally honest. As you continue your exploration, be sure to add to your list any additional values that occur to you.

STEP 3: Calculating Your Economic Needs

Each of us grew up in an environment that provided for certain basic needs, such as food and shelter, and, to varying degrees, other needs that we now consider basic, such as cable TV, reading materials, or an automobile. Needs such as privacy, space, and quiet, which at first glance may not appear to be monetary needs, may add to housing expenses and so should be considered as you examine your economic needs. For example, if you place a high value on a large, open living space for yourself, it would be difficult to satisfy that need without an associated high housing cost, especially in a densely populated city environment.

As you prepare to move into the world of work and become responsible for meeting your own basic needs, it is important to consider the salary you will need to be able to afford a satisfying standard of living. The three-step process outlined here will help you plan a budget, which in turn will allow you to evaluate the various career choices and geographic locations you are considering. The steps include (1) developing a realistic budget, (2) examining starting salaries, and (3) using a cost-of-living index.

Developing a Realistic Budget. Each of us has certain expectations for the kind of lifestyle we want to maintain. In order to begin the process of defining your economic needs, it will be helpful to determine what you expect to spend on routine monthly expenses. These expenses include housing, food, transportation, entertainment, utilities, loan repayments, and revolving charge accounts. A worksheet that details many of these expenses is shown in Exhibit 1.4. You may not currently spend for certain items, but you probably

---

Exhibit 1.4

Estimated Monthly Expenses Worksheet

		Could reduce spending? (Yes/No)
Cable	$ _____	_____
Child care	_____	_____

		Could reduce spending? (Yes/No)
Clothing	_____	_____
Educational loan repayment	_____	_____
Entertainment	_____	_____
Food		
At home	_____	_____
Meals out	_____	_____
Gifts	_____	_____
Housing		
Rent/mortgage	_____	_____
Insurance	_____	_____
Property taxes	_____	_____
Medical insurance	_____	_____
Reading materials		
Newspapers	_____	_____
Magazines	_____	_____
Books	_____	_____
Revolving loans/charges	_____	_____
Savings	_____	_____
Telephone	_____	_____
Transportation		
Auto payment	_____	_____
Insurance	_____	_____
Parking	_____	_____
Gasoline	_____	_____
or		
Cab/train/bus fare	_____	_____
Utilities		
Electric	_____	_____
Gas	_____	_____
Water/sewer	_____	_____
Vacations	_____	_____
Miscellaneous expense 1	_____	_____
Expense: _____		
Miscellaneous expense 2	_____	_____
Expense: _____		
Miscellaneous expense 3	_____	_____
Expense: _____		

TOTAL MONTHLY EXPENSES:_____

YEARLY EXPENSES (Monthly expenses x 12): _____

INCREASE TO INCLUDE TAXES (Yearly expenses x 1.35): ____ =

MINIMUM ANNUAL SALARY REQUIREMENT _____

will have to once you begin supporting yourself. As you develop this budget, be generous in your estimates, but keep in mind any items that could be reduced or eliminated. If you are not sure about the cost of a certain item, talk with family or friends who would be able to give you a realistic estimate.

If budgeting is new or difficult for you, start to keep a log of expenses right now. You may be surprised at how much you actually spend each month for food or stamps or magazines. Household expenses and personal grooming items can often loom very large in a budget, as can auto repairs or home maintenance.

Income taxes must also be taken into consideration when examining salary requirements. State and local taxes vary by location, so it is difficult to calculate exactly the effect of taxes on the amount of income you need to generate. To roughly estimate the gross income necessary to generate your minimum annual salary requirement, multiply the minimum salary you have calculated (see Exhibit 1.4) by a factor of 1.35. The resulting figure will be an approximation of what your gross income would need to be, given your estimated expenses.

Examining Starting Salaries. Starting salaries for each of the career tracks are provided throughout this book. These salary figures can be used in conjunction with the cost-of-living index (discussed in the next section) to determine whether you would be able to meet your basic economic needs in a given geographic location.

Using a Cost-of-Living Index. If you are thinking about trying to get a job in a geographic region other than the one where you now live, understanding differences in the cost of living will help you come to a more informed decision about making a move. By using a cost-of-living index, you can compare salaries offered and the cost of living in different locations with what you know about the salaries offered and the cost of living in your present location.

Many variables are used to calculate the cost-of-living index, including housing expenses, groceries, utilities, transportation, health care, clothing, entertainment, local income taxes, and local sales taxes. Cost-of-living indices can be found in many resources, such as *Equal Employment Opportunity Bimonthly, Places Rated Almanac,* or *The Best Towns in America.* They are constantly being recalculated based on changes in costs.

· ·

If you lived in Cleveland, Ohio, for example, and you were interested in working as a high school economics teacher, you would earn, on average, $37,835 annually.

But let's say you're also thinking about moving to either New York, Los Angeles, or Denver. You know you can live on $37,835 in Cleveland, but you want to be able to compare that salary to salaries in other locations.

Job: High School Economics Teacher

CITY	INDEX	EQUIVALENT SALARY

$$\frac{\text{New York}}{\text{Cleveland}} \quad \frac{213.3}{114.3} \times \$37,835 = \$70,605 \text{ in New York}$$

$$\frac{\text{Los Angeles}}{\text{Cleveland}} \quad \frac{124.6}{114.3} \times \$37,835 = \$41,244 \text{ in Los Angeles}$$

$$\frac{\text{Denver}}{\text{Cleveland}} \quad \frac{100.0}{114.3} \times \$37,835 = \$33,101 \text{ in Denver}$$

You would have to earn $70,605 in New York, $41,244 in Los Angeles, or $33,101 in Denver to match the buying power of $37,835 in Cleveland.

If you would like to determine whether it's financially worthwhile to make any of these moves, one more piece of information is needed: the actual average salaries of high school economics teachers in New York, Los Angeles, and Denver. *The American Salaries and Wages Survey* (4th edition) reports the following average salary information for high school social science teachers (which includes high school economics teachers):

City	Annual Salary	Salary Equivalent to Ohio	Change in Buying Power
New York	$48,115	$70,605	−$22,490
Los Angeles	$43,114	$41,244	+$ 1,870
Denver	$35,364	$33,101	+$ 2,263
Cleveland	$37,835	—	—

If you moved to New York City and secured employment as a high school economics teacher, you would not be able to maintain a lifestyle similar to the one you led in Cleveland; in fact, you would have to add more than

> 50 percent to your income to maintain a similar lifestyle in New York. The same would not be true for a move to Los Angeles or Denver. You would increase your buying power given the rate of pay and cost of living in these cities.

....

You can work through a similar exercise for any type of job you are considering and for many locations when current salary information is available. It is worth your time to undertake this analysis if you are seriously considering a relocation. By doing so, you will be able to make an informed choice.

STEP 4:   Exploring Your Longer-Term Goals

There is no question that when we first begin working, our goals are to use our skills and education in a job that will reward us with employment, income, and status relative to the preparation we brought with us to this position. If we are not being paid as much as we feel we should for our level of education, or if job demands don't provide the intellectual stimulation we had hoped for, we experience unhappiness and as a result often seek other employment.

Most jobs we consider "good" are those that fulfill our basic "lower-level" needs of security, food, clothing, shelter, income, and productive work. But even when our basic needs are met and our jobs are secure and productive, we as individuals are constantly changing. As we change, the demands and expectations we place on our jobs may change. Fortunately, some jobs grow and change with us, and this explains why some people are happy through-out many years in a job.

But more often people are bigger than the jobs they fill. We have more goals and needs than any job could fulfill. These are "higher-level" needs of self-esteem, companionship, affection, and an increasing desire to feel we are employing ourselves in the most effective way possible. Not all of these higher-level needs can be fulfilled through employment, but for as long as we are employed, we increasingly demand that our jobs play their part in moving us along the path to fulfillment.

Another obvious but important fact is that we change as we mature. Although our jobs also have the potential for change, they may not change as frequently or as markedly as we do. There are increasingly fewer one-job, one-employer careers; we must think about a work future that may involve voluntary or forced moves from employer to employer. Because of that very real possibility, we need to take advantage of the opportunities in each position we hold to acquire skills and competencies that will keep us viable and attractive as employees in a job market that is not only increasingly technology/computer dependent, but also is populated with more and more small, self-transforming organizations rather than the large, seemingly stable organizations of the past.

It may be difficult in the early stages of the job search to determine whether the path you are considering can meet these longer-term goals. Reading about career paths and individual career histories in your field can be very helpful in this regard. Meeting and talking with individuals further along in their careers can be enlightening as well. Older workers can provide valuable guidance on "self-managing" your career, which will become an increasingly valuable skill in the future. Some of these ideas may seem remote as you read this now, but you should be able to appreciate the need to ensure that you are growing, developing valuable new skills, and researching other employers who might be interested in your particular skills package.

> **If you are considering a position as an urban planner, for example, you would gain a better perspective on this career if you talked to an entry-level planning assistant, a more senior and experienced town planner or city planner, and finally a director of planning for a city, town, or county who has had a considerable work history in urban planning. Each will have a different perspective, unique concerns, and an individual set of value priorities.**

STEP 5: Enumerating Your Skill Base

In terms of the job search, skills can be thought of as capabilities that can be developed in school, at work, or by volunteering and then used in specific job settings. Many studies have documented the kinds of skills that employers seek in entry-level applicants. For example, some of the most desired skills for individuals interested in the teaching profession include the ability to interact effectively with students one on one, to manage a classroom, to adapt to varying situations as necessary, and to get involved in school activities. Business employers have also identified important qualities, including enthusiasm for the employer's product or service, a businesslike mind, the ability to follow written or verbal instructions, the ability to demonstrate self-control, the confidence to suggest new ideas, the ability to communicate with all members of a group, awareness of cultural differences, and loyalty, to name just a few. You will find that many of these skills are also in the repertoire of qualities demanded in your college major.

In order to be successful in obtaining any given job, you must be able to demonstrate that you possess a certain mix of skills that will allow you to carry out the duties required by that job. This skill mix will vary a great deal from job to job; to determine the skills necessary for the jobs you are seeking, you can read job advertisements or more generic job descriptions, such as those found later in this book. If you want to be effective in the job search, you must directly show employers that you possess the skills needed to be successful in filling the position. These skills will initially be described on your resume and then discussed again during the interview process.

Skills are either general or specific. General skills are those that are developed throughout the college years by taking classes, being employed, and getting involved in other related activities such as volunteer work or campus organizations. General skills include the ability to read and write, to perform computations, to think critically, and to communicate effectively. Specific skills are also acquired on the job and in the classroom, but they allow you to complete tasks that require specialized knowledge. Computer programming, drafting, language translating, and copyediting are just a few examples of specific skills that may relate to a given job.

In order to develop a list of skills relevant to employers, you must first identify the general skills you possess, then list specific skills you have to offer, and, finally, examine which of these skills employers are seeking.

Identifying Your General Skills. Because you possess or will possess a college degree, employers will assume that you can read and write, perform certain basic computations, think critically, and communicate effectively. Employers will want to see that you have acquired these skills, and they will want to know which additional general skills you possess.

One way to begin identifying skills is to write an experiential diary. An experiential diary lists all the tasks you were responsible for completing for each job you've held and then outlines the skills required to do those tasks. You may list several skills for any given task. This diary allows you to distinguish between the tasks you performed and the underlying skills required to complete those tasks. Here's an example:

Tasks	Skills
Answering telephone	Effective use of language, clear diction, ability to direct inquiries, ability to solve problems
Waiting on tables	Poise under conditions of time and pressure, speed, accuracy, good memory, simultaneous completion of tasks, sales skills

For each job or experience you have participated in, develop a worksheet based on the example shown here. On a resume, you may want to describe these skills rather than simply listing tasks. Skills are easier for the employer to appreciate, especially when your experience is very different from the employment you are seeking. In addition to helping you identify general skills, this experiential diary will prepare you to speak more effectively in an interview about the qualifications you possess.

Identifying Your Specific Skills. It may be easier to identify your specific skills because you can definitely say whether you can speak other languages, program a computer, draft a map or diagram, or edit a document using appropriate symbols and terminology.

Using your experiential diary, identify the points in your history where you learned how to do something very specific, and decide whether you have a beginning, intermediate, or advanced knowledge of how to use that particular skill. Right now, be sure to list *every* specific skill you have, and don't consider whether you like using the skill. Write down a list of specific skills you have acquired and the level of competence you possess—beginning, intermediate, or advanced.

Relating Your Skills to Employers. You probably have thought about a couple of different jobs you might be interested in obtaining, and one way to begin relating the general and specific skills you possess to a potential employer's needs is to read actual advertisements for these types of positions (see Part Two for resources listing actual job openings).

....

For example, you might be interested in working as an economic analyst for a government agency that deals with foreign trade, prior to returning to graduate school to seek a master's degree in international relations with a specialty in economics. A typical job listing might read, "conduct trade policy analysis, economic evaluations, and import-export studies. Bachelor's degree in economics, international business, or political science required. International experience preferred." If you then used any one of a number of sources of information that described the job of policy analyst or international trade specialist, you would find additional information. Policy analysts in this area track and report on trade laws and policies, interpret laws and regulations, and advise senior managers about economic and political policies.

Begin building a comprehensive list of required skills with the first job description you read. Exploring advertisements for several types of related positions will reveal an important core of skills necessary for obtaining the type of work you're interested in. Include both general and specific skills.

Following is a sample list of skills needed to be successful as a policy analyst in international trade.

Job: International trade policy analyst

General Skills	Specific Skills
Accounting	Estimating trade volume
Reading	Tracking development of foreign legislation related to trade
Gathering information	Compiling trade figures
Making decisions	Evaluating alternatives
Meeting deadlines	Preparing reports
Attending meetings	Communicating recommendations for policy changes
Entering data into computer	Preparing quarterly trade summaries
Writing	Editing trade reports

On separate sheets of paper, try to generate a list of required skills for at least one job you are considering.

The list of general skills that you develop for a given career path would be valuable for any number of jobs you might seek. Many specific skills would also be transferable to other types of positions. For example, editing reports is a required skill for other types of analysts and for almost any management position. The ability to use basic word processing and spreadsheet software would also be useful in almost any job setting.

. . . .

Now review the list of skills you developed and check off those skills that *you know you possess* and that are required for jobs you are considering. You should refer to these specific skills on the resume that you write for this type of job. See Chapter 2 for details on resume writing.

STEP 6: Recognizing Your Preferred Skills

In the previous section you developed a comprehensive list of skills that relate to particular career paths that are of interest to you. You can now relate these to skills that you prefer to use. We all use a wide range of skills (some researchers say individuals have a repertoire of about five hundred skills), but we may not be particularly interested in using all of them in our work. There may be some skills that come to us more naturally or that we use successfully time and time again and that we want to continue to use; these are best described as our preferred skills. For this exercise use the list of skills that you developed for the previous section and decide which of them you are *most interested in using* in future work and how often you would like to use them. You might be interested in using some skills only occasionally, while others you would like to use more regularly. You probably also have skills that you hope you can use constantly.

As you examine job announcements, look for matches between this list of preferred skills and the qualifications described in the advertisements. These skills should be highlighted on your resume and discussed in job interviews.

STEP 7: Assessing Skills Needing Further Development

Previously you developed a list of general and specific skills required for given positions. You already possess some of these skills; those that remain to be developed are your underdeveloped skills.

If you are just beginning the job search, there may be gaps between the qualifications required for some of the jobs being considered and skills you possess. These are your underdeveloped skills. The thought of having to admit to and talk about these underdeveloped skills, especially in a job interview, is a frightening one. One way to put a healthy perspective on this subject is to target and relate your exploration of underdeveloped skills to the types of positions you are seeking. Recognizing these shortcomings and planning to overcome them with either on-the-job training or additional formal education can be a positive way to address the concept of underdeveloped skills.

On your worksheet or in your journal, make a list of up to five general or specific skills required for the positions you're interested in that you *don't currently possess.* For each item, list an idea you have for specific action you could take to acquire that skill. Do some brainstorming to come up with possible actions. If you have a hard time generating ideas, talk to people currently working in this type of position, professionals in your college career services office, trusted friends, family members, or members of related professional associations.

If, for example, you are interested in a job for which you don't have some specific required experience, you could locate training opportunities such as classes or workshops offered through a local college or university, community college, or club or association that would help you build the level of expertise you need for the job.

Many excellent jobs in today's economy demand computer skills you probably already have. Most graduates are not so lucky and have to acquire these skills—often before an employer will give their application serious consideration. So, what can you do if you find there are certain skills you're missing? If you're still in school, try to fill the gaps in your knowledge before you graduate. If you've already graduated, look at evening programs, continuing education courses, or tutorial programs that may be available commercially. Developing a modest level of expertise will encourage you to be more confident in suggesting to potential employers that you can continue to add to your skill base on the job.

In Chapter 5 on interviewing, we will discuss in detail how to effectively address questions about underdeveloped skills. Generally speaking, though, employers want genuine answers to these types of questions. They want you to reveal "the real you," and they also want to see how you answer difficult questions. In taking the positive, targeted approach discussed above, you show the employer that you are willing to continue to learn and that you have a plan for strengthening your job qualifications.

USING YOUR SELF-ASSESSMENT

Exploring entry-level career options can be an exciting experience if you have good resources available and will take the time to use them. Can you effectively complete the following tasks?

1. Understand and relate your personality traits to career choices.

2. Define your personal values.

3. Determine your economic needs.

4. Explore longer-term goals.

5. Understand your skill base.

6. Recognize your preferred skills.

7. Express a willingness to improve on your underdeveloped skills.

If so, then you can more meaningfully participate in the job search process by writing a more effective resume, finding job titles that represent work you are interested in doing, locating job sites that will provide the opportunity for you to use your strengths and skills, networking in an informed way, participating in focused interviews, getting the most out of follow-up contacts, and evaluating job offers to find those that create a good match between you and the employer.

The remaining chapters in Part One guide you through these next steps in the job search process. For many job seekers, this process can take anywhere from three months to a year to implement. The time you will need to put into your job search will depend on the type of job you want and the geographic location where you'd like to work. Think of your effort as a job in itself, requiring you to set aside time each week to complete the needed work. Carefully undertaken efforts may reduce the time you need for your job search.

CHAPTER TWO

THE RESUME AND COVER LETTER

The task of writing a resume may seem overwhelming if you are unfamiliar with this type of document, but there are some easily understood techniques that can and should be used. This section was written to help you understand the purpose of the resume, the different types of resume formats available, and how to write the sections of information traditionally found on a resume. We will present examples and explanations that address questions frequently posed by people writing their first resume or updating an old resume.

Even within the formats and suggestions given below, however, there are infinite variations. True, most resumes follow one of the outlines suggested below, but you should feel free to adjust the resume to suit your needs and make it expressive of your life and experience.

WHY WRITE A RESUME?

The purpose of a resume is to convince an employer that you should be interviewed. You'll want to present enough information to show that you can make an immediate and valuable contribution to an organization. A resume is not an in-depth historical or legal document; later in the job search process you'll be asked to document your entire work history on an application form and attest to its validity. The resume should, instead, highlight relevant information pertaining directly to the organization that will receive the document or the type of position you are seeking.

We will discuss four types of resumes in this chapter: chronological resume, functional resume, targeted resume, and the broadcast letter. The reasons for using one type of resume over another and the typical format for each are addressed in the following sections.

THE CHRONOLOGICAL RESUME

The chronological resume is the most common of the various resume formats and therefore the format that employers are most used to receiving. This type of resume is easy to read and understand because it details the chronological progression of jobs you have held. (See Exhibit 2.1.) It begins with your most recent employment and works back in time. If you have a solid work history or have experience that provided growth and development in your duties and responsibilities, a chronological resume will highlight these achievements. The typical elements of a chronological resume include the heading, a career objective, educational background, employment experience, activities, and references.

The Heading

The heading consists of your name, address, telephone number, fax number, and E-mail address. We suggest that you spell out your full name and type it in all capital letters in bold type. After all, you are the focus of the resume! If you have a current as well as a permanent address and you include both in the heading, be sure to indicate until what date your current address will be valid. Don't forget to include the zip code with your address and the area code with your telephone number.

The Objective

As you formulate the wording for this part of your resume, keep the following points in mind.

The Objective Focuses the Resume. Without a doubt this is the most challenging part of the resume for most resume writers. Even for individuals who have quite firmly decided on a career path, it can be difficult to encapsulate all they want to say in one or two brief sentences. For job seekers who are unfocused or unclear about their intentions, trying to write this section can inhibit the entire resume writing process.

Recruiters tell us, time and again, that the objective creates a frame of reference for them. It helps them see how you express your goals and career focus. In addition, the statement may indicate in what ways you can

Exhibit 2.1

Chronological Resume

JOHN RAVINE
345 Duke Street
Apartment 3B
Albuquerque, NM 87110
(505) 555-7500

OBJECTIVE
Interested in a position teaching economics, in a public or private high school setting.

EDUCATION
Bachelor of Science
University of New Mexico
Albuquerque, NM
May 2000
Major: Economics
Minor: Teacher Education

Honors/Activities: Vice President of Student Government
Association
President, Economics Club
Member, Student Ambassadors
Dean's List four semesters, President's List
three semesters
Magna cum laude graduate

EXPERIENCE
Peer Tutor: University of New Mexico Academic Assistance Center
Academic Year 1999–2000
Provided tutoring in a variety of subjects to freshman experiencing academic difficulty.

Research Assistant: University of New Mexico Economics Department
Academic Years 1998–2000
Assisted economics professor designing market survey questionnaires and conducting interviews.

> **Youth Counselor: YMCA, Albuquerque, NM**
> Academic Years 1997–1999
> In a work-study position, planned and supervised youth activities, taught swimming, and performed lifeguarding duties.
>
> **Intern: New Mexico Political Action Center**
> Summer 1997
> Assisted in compiling election data and completing reports regarding voter preferences.
>
> ### COMMUNITY SERVICE
> Active volunteer with Albuquerque Historical Society; election day poll worker; volunteer Big Brother.
>
> ### REFERENCES
> Both personal and professional references are available upon request.

immediately benefit an organization. Given the importance of the objective, every point covered in the resume should relate to it. If information doesn't relate, it should be omitted. With the word-processing technology available today, each resume can and should be tailored for individual employers or specific positions that are available. Thus, you may create several different resumes, each tailored to a certain type of job.

Choose an Appropriate Length. Because of the brevity necessary for a resume, you should keep the objective as short as possible. Although objectives of only four or five words often don't show much direction, objectives that take three full lines could be viewed as too wordy and might possibly be ignored.

Consider Which Type of Objective Statement You Will Use. There are many ways to state an objective, but generally there are four forms this statement can take: (1) a very general statement; (2) a statement focused on a specific position; (3) a statement focused on a specific industry; or (4) a summary of your qualifications. In our contacts with employers, we often hear that many resumes don't exhibit any direction or career goals, so we suggest avoiding general statements when possible.

1. General Objective Statement. General objective statements look like the following:

- An entry-level educational programming coordinator position
- An entry-level marketing position

This type of objective is useful if you know what type of job you want but you're not sure which industries interest you.

2. *Position-Focused Objective.* Following are examples of objectives focusing on a specific position:

- ❑ To obtain the position of director of public information at the State Council for Environmental Quality
- ❑ To obtain a position as assistant town manager

When a student applies for an advertised job opening, this type of focus can be very effective. The employer knows that the applicant has taken the time to tailor the resume specifically for this position.

3. *Industry-Focused Objective.* Focusing on a particular industry in an objective could be stated as follows:

- ❑ To begin a career as a sales representative in the cruise line industry

4. *Summary of Qualifications Statement.* The summary of qualifications can be used instead of an objective or in conjunction with an objective. The purpose of this type of statement is to highlight relevant qualifications gained through a variety of experiences. This type of statement is often used by individuals with extensive and diversified work experience. An example of a qualifications statement follows:

· ·

A degree in economics and four years of progressively increasing job responsibility in a regional planning office have prepared me to begin a career as a manager in a government agency where thoroughness and attention to detail are valued.

· ·

Support Your Objective. A resume that contains any one of these types of objective statements should then go on to demonstrate why you are qualified to get the position. Listing academic degrees can be one way to indicate qualifications. Another demonstration would be in the way previous experiences, both volunteer and paid, are described. Without this kind of documentation in the body of the resume, the objective looks unsupported.

Think of the resume as telling a connected story about you. All the elements should work together to form a coherent picture that ideally should relate to your statement of objective.

Education

This section of your resume should indicate the exact name of the degree you will receive or have received, spelled out completely with no abbreviations. The degree is generally listed after the objective, followed by the institution name and address, and then the month and year of graduation. This section could also include your academic minor, grade point average (GPA), and appearance on the Dean's List or President's List.

If you have enough space, you might want to include a section listing courses related to the field in which you are seeking work. The best use of a "related courses" section would be to list some course work that is not traditionally associated with the major. Perhaps you took several computer courses outside your degree that will be helpful and related to the job prospects you are entertaining. Several education section examples are shown here:

••••••••••••••••••••••••••••••••••••••

❑ **Bachelor of Arts Degree in Economics**
University of Florida, Gainesville, FL, 2000
Minor: Political Science

❑ **Bachelor of Science Degree with Major in**
Economics
Boston University, Boston, MA, May 2000
Minor: History

❑ **Bachelor of Science Degree in Economics**
University of Denver, Denver, CO, 2000
Concentration: Finance

An example of a format for a related courses section follows:

RELATED COURSES	
Accounting	Auditing
Computer Science	Spanish
Market Research	Research Methods

••••••••••••••••••••••••••••••••••••••

Experience

The experience section of your resume should be the most substantial part and should take up most of the space on the page. Employers want to see what kind of work history you have. They will look at your range of experiences, longevity in jobs, and specific tasks you are able to complete. This section may also be called "work experience," "related experience," "employment history," or "employment." No matter what you call this section, some important points to remember are the following:

1. **Describe your duties** as they relate to the position you are seeking.

2. **Emphasize major responsibilities** and indicate increases in responsibility. Include all relevant employment experiences: summer, part-time, internships, cooperative education, or self-employment.

3. **Emphasize skills**, especially those that transfer from one situation to another. The fact that you coordinated a student organization, chaired meetings, supervised others, and managed a budget leads one to suspect that you could coordinate other things as well.

4. **Use descriptive job titles** that provide information about what you did. A "Student Intern" should be more specifically stated as, for example, "Magazine Operations Intern." "Volunteer" is also too general; a title like "Peer Writing Tutor" would be more appropriate.

5. **Create word pictures** by using active verbs to start sentences. Describe *results* you have produced in the work you have done.

A limp description would say something like the following: "My duties included helping with production, proofreading, and editing. I used a word-processing package to alter text." An action statement would be stated as follows: "Coordinated and assisted in the creative marketing of brochures and seminar promotions, becoming proficient in WordPerfect."

Remember, an accomplishment is simply a result, a final measurable product that people can relate to. A duty is not a result, it is an obligation—every job holder has duties. For an effective resume, list as many results as you can. To make the most of the limited space you have and to give your description impact, carefully select appropriate and accurate descriptors from the list of action words in Exhibit 2.2.

Here are some traits/experiences that employers tell us they like to see:

- ❏ Teamwork
- ❏ Energy and motivation
- ❏ Learning and using new skills
- ❏ Demonstrated versatility

- Critical thinking
- Understanding how profits are created
- Displaying organizational acumen
- Communicating directly and clearly, in both writing and speaking
- Taking risks
- Willingness to admit mistakes
- Manifesting high personal standards

Exhibit 2.2

Resume Action Verbs

Achieved	Created	Illustrated
Acted	Decreased	Implemented
Administered	Defined	Improved
Advised	Demonstrated	Increased
Analyzed	Designed	Influenced
Assessed	Determined	Informed
Assisted	Developed	Initiated
Attained	Directed	Innovated
Balanced	Documented	Instituted
Budgeted	Drafted	Instructed
Calculated	Edited	Integrated
Collected	Eliminated	Interpreted
Communicated	Ensured	Introduced
Compiled	Established	Learned
Completed	Estimated	Lectured
Composed	Evaluated	Led
Conceptualized	Examined	Maintained
Condensed	Explained	Managed
Conducted	Facilitated	Mapped
Consolidated	Finalized	Marketed
Constructed	Generated	Met
Controlled	Handled	Modified
Converted	Headed	Monitored
Coordinated	Helped	Negotiated
Corrected	Identified	Observed

continued

continued

Obtained	Questioned	Simplified
Operated	Realized	Sketched
Organized	Received	Sold
Participated	Recommended	Solved
Performed	Recorded	Staffed
Planned	Reduced	Streamlined
Predicted	Reinforced	Studied
Prepared	Reported	Submitted
Presented	Represented	Summarized
Processed	Researched	Systematized
Produced	Resolved	Tabulated
Projected	Reviewed	Tested
Proposed	Scheduled	Transacted
Provided	Selected	Updated
Qualified	Served	Verified
Quantified	Showed	Wrote

SOLUTIONS TO FREQUENTLY ENCOUNTERED PROBLEMS

Repetitive Employment with the Same Employer

EMPLOYMENT: The Foot Locker, Portland, Oregon. Summer 1997, 1998, 1999. Initially employed in high school as salesclerk. Due to successful performance, asked to return next two summers at higher pay with added responsibility. Ranked as the #2 salesperson the first summer and #1 the next two summers. Assisted in arranging eye-catching retail displays; served as manager of other summer workers during owner's absence.

A Large Number of Jobs

EMPLOYMENT: Recent Hospitality Industry Experience: Affiliated with four upscale hotel/restaurant complexes (September 1996–February 1999), where I worked part- and full-time as a waiter, bartender, disc jockey, and bookkeeper to produce income for college.

Several Positions with the Same Employer

EMPLOYMENT: Coca-Cola Bottling Co., Burlington, Vermont, 1996–1999. In four years, I received three promotions, each with increased pay and responsibility.

Summer Sales Coordinator: Promoted to hire, train, and direct efforts of add-on staff of fifteen college-age route salespeople hired to meet summer peak demand for product.

Sales Administrator: Promoted to run home office sales desk, managing accounts and associated delivery schedules for professional sales force of ten people. Included intensive phone work, daily interaction with all personnel, and strong knowledge of product line.

Route Salesperson: Summer employment to travel and tourism industry sites using Coke products. Met specific schedule demands, used good communication skills with wide variety of customers, and demonstrated strong selling skills. Named Salesperson of the Month for July and August of that year.

QUESTIONS RESUME WRITERS OFTEN ASK

How Far Back Should I Go in Terms of Listing Past Jobs?

Usually, listing three or four jobs should suffice. If you did something back in high school that has a bearing on your future aspirations for employment, however, by all means list the job. As you progress through your college career, high school jobs may be replaced on the resume by college employment.

Should I Differentiate Between Paid and Nonpaid Employment?

Most employers are not initially concerned about how much you were paid. They are anxious to know how much responsibility you held in your past employment. There is no need to specify that your work was volunteer if you had significant responsibilities.

How Should I Represent My Accomplishments or Work-Related Responsibilities?

Succinctly, but fully. In other words, give the employer enough information to arouse curiosity, but not so much detail that you leave nothing to the imagination. Besides, some jobs merit more lengthy explanations than others. Be sure to convey any information that can give an employer a better understanding of the depth of your involvement at work. Did you supervise others? How many? Did your efforts result in a more efficient operation? How much did you increase efficiency? Did you handle a budget? How much? Were you promoted in a short time? Did you work two jobs at once or fifteen hours per week after high school? Where appropriate, quantify.

Should the Work Section Always Follow the Education Section on the Resume?

Always lead with your strengths. If your education closely relates to the employment you now seek, put this section after the objective. Or, if you are weak on the academic side but have a surplus of good work experiences, consider reversing the order of your sections to lead with employment, followed by education.

How Should I Present My Activities, Honors, Awards, Professional Societies, and Affiliations?

This section of the resume can add valuable information for an employer to consider if used correctly. The rule of thumb for information in this section is to include only those activities that are in some way relevant to the objective stated on your resume. If you can draw a valid connection between your activities and your objective, include them; if not, leave them out.

Granted, this is hard to do. Playing center on the championship basketball team or serving as coordinator of the biggest homecoming parade ever held are roles that have meaning for you and represent personal accomplishments you'd like to share. But the resume is a brief document, and the information you provide on it should help the employer make a decision about your job eligibility. Including personal details can be confusing and could hurt your candidacy. Limiting your activity list to a few very significant experiences can be very effective.

If you are applying for a position as a safety officer, your certificate in Red Cross lifesaving skills or CPR would be related and valuable. You would want to include it. If, however, you are applying for a job as a junior account executive in an advertising agency, that information would be unrelated and superfluous. Leave it out.

Professional affiliations and honors should *all* be listed; especially important are those related to your job objective. Social clubs and activities need not be a part of your resume unless you hold a significant office or you are looking for a position related to your membership. Be aware that most prospective employers' principle concerns are related to your employability, not your social life. If you have any, publications can be included as an addendum to your resume.

The focus of the resume is your experience and education. It is not necessary to describe your involvement in activities. However, if your resume needs to be lengthened, this section provides the freedom either to expand on or mention only briefly the contributions you have made. If you have made significant contributions (e.g., an officer of an organization or a particularly long tenure with a group), you may choose to describe them in more detail.

It is not always necessary to include the dates of your memberships with your activities the way you would include job dates.

There are a number of different ways in which to present additional information. You may give this section a number of different titles. Assess what you want to list, and then use an appropriate title. Do not use "extracurricular activities." This terminology is scholastic, not professional, and therefore not appropriate. The following are two examples:

- ACTIVITIES: Society for Technical Communication, Student Senate, Student Admissions Representative, Senior Class Officer

- ACTIVITIES:
  - Society for Technical Communication Member
  - Student Senator
  - Student Admissions Representative
  - Senior Class Officer

The position you are looking for will determine what you should or should not include. *Always* look for a correlation between the activity and the prospective job.

How Should I Handle References?

The use of references is considered a part of the interview process, and they should never be listed on a resume. You would always provide references to a potential employer if requested to, so it is not even necessary to include this section on the resume if room does not permit. If space is available, it is acceptable to include one of the following statements:

- REFERENCES: Furnished upon request.

- REFERENCES: Available upon request.

Individuals used as references must be protected from unnecessary contacts. By including names on your resume, you leave your references unprotected. Overuse and abuse of your references will lead to less-than-supportive comments. Protect your references by giving out their names only when you are being considered seriously as a candidate for a given position.

THE FUNCTIONAL RESUME

The functional resume departs from a chronological resume in that it organizes information by specific accomplishments in various settings: previous

Exhibit 2.3

Functional Resume

CAROL ZELLICK

23 Pinyon Street
Phoenix, AZ 85032
(602) 555-1222 (voice)
(602) 555-2358 (fax)
E-mail: Czell234@aol.com

OBJECTIVE
Seeking an entry-level position in public service, international affairs, or a related area. Particularly interested in public relations/public affairs.

CAPABILITIES/ATTRIBUTES
- High energy, task oriented, decision maker
- Excellent quantitative and analytical skills
- Fluent in French
- Interested and well-informed in international affairs
- Strong written and verbal skills
- Strong people skills
- Experienced international traveler
- Strong computer skills

SELECTED EXPERIENCE/ACCOMPLISHMENTS
Public Relations: Through a college work-study program, I achieved four years of progressively more challenging duties in the public relations department of a major political campaign. Created copy and designed layout for promotional material. Worked on brochures and flyers. Manned phone banks. Scheduled campaign activities.
Teamwork: Collaborated with coworkers and professionals in a variety of campaign-related duties.
Leadership: Supervised volunteers working on campaign mailings.
Awards: Graduated with honors in economics.

EMPLOYMENT HISTORY
Intern, Arizona Trade Authority, Summer 1998
Telemarketer, Police Benevolent Fund, Tucson, Arizona, Summer
1996 and 1997

EDUCATION
Bachelor of Arts, University of Arizona
Tuscon, Arizona
May 2000
Major: Economics
Minor: Political Science

REFERENCES
Provided upon request

jobs, volunteer work, associations, etc. This type of resume permits you to stress the substance of your experiences rather than the position titles you have held. (See Exhibit 2.3.) You should consider using a functional resume if you have held a series of similar jobs that relied on the same skills or abilities.

The Objective

A functional resume begins with an objective that can be used to focus the contents of the resume.

Specific Accomplishments

Specific accomplishments are listed on this type of resume. Examples of the types of headings used to describe these capabilities might include sales, counseling, teaching, communication, production, management, marketing, or writing. The headings you choose will directly relate to your experience and the tasks that you carried out. Each accomplishment section contains statements related to your experience in that category, regardless of when or where it occurred. Organize the accomplishments and the related tasks you describe in their order of importance as related to the position you seek.

Experience or Employment History

Your actual work experience is condensed and placed after the specific accomplishments section. It simply lists dates of employment, position titles, and employer names.

Education

The education section of a functional resume is identical to that of the chronological resume, but it does not carry the same visual importance because it is placed near the bottom of the page.

References

Because actual reference names are never listed on a resume, this section is optional if space does not permit.

THE TARGETED RESUME

The targeted resume focuses on specific work-related capabilities you can bring to a given position within an organization. (See Exhibit 2.4.) It should be sent to an individual within the organization who makes hiring decisions about the position you are seeking.

The Objective

The objective on this type of resume should be targeted to a specific career or position. It should be supported by the capabilities, accomplishments, and achievements documented in the resume.

Exhibit 2.4

Targeted Resume

DEBBIE GOODMAN

Monument Hall, Room 250	4470 Maple Drive
Case Western Reserve University	Columbus, OH 43229
Cleveland, OH 44114	(614) 555-2359
(216) 555-0321	
(Until May 2000)	

JOB TARGET
Planning assistant with a state or regional planning agency

CAPABILITIES
- Collect and analyze data
- Review and revise reports and planning documents
- Have proven team skills

- Work under broad supervision
- Am familiar with a variety of computer software

ACHIEVEMENTS
- Codeveloped peer counseling program
- Placed several editorials in local newspapers
- Graduated with honors

WORK HISTORY

1998–present   Administrative Assistant, Cleveland Urban Planning Office, Cleveland, Ohio
- Work-study position assisting the chief planner, analyzing data, writing and reviewing reports.

1997–1998   Student Assistant, Department of Economics, Case Western Reserve University, Cleveland, Ohio
- Assisted department head with general office duties. Also conducted background research for grant-funded project on economic trends in nineteenth-century United States.

EDUCATION
Bachelor of Arts in Economics
Case Western Reserve University
2000

REFERENCES ON REQUEST

Capabilities

Capabilities should be statements that illustrate tasks you believe you are capable of based on your accomplishments, achievements, and work history. Each should relate to your targeted career or position. You can stress your qualifications rather than your employment history. This approach may require research to obtain an understanding of the nature of the work involved and the capabilities necessary to carry out that work.

Accomplishments/Achievements

This section relates the various activities you have been involved in to the job market. These experiences may include previous jobs, extracurricular activities at school, internships, and part-time summer work.

Experience

Your work history should be listed in abbreviated form and may include position title, employer name, and employment dates.

Education

Because this type of resume is directed toward a specific job target and an individual's related experience, the education section is not prominently located at the top of the resume as is done on the chronological resume.

THE BROADCAST LETTER

The broadcast letter is used by some job seekers in place of a resume and cover letter. (See Exhibit 2.5.) The purpose of this type of document is to

---

Exhibit 2.5

Broadcast Letter

DAN CONRAD
4466 Southern Blvd.
Rio Rancho, NM 87166
(505) 555-2145

July 27, 2000

Mr. Gordon Newman
Personnel Director
Bank of New Mexico
Albuquerque, NM 87122

Dear Mr. Newman,

As a recent graduate with a bachelor's degree in economics from the University of New Mexico, I have had the opportunity to work in several bank settings in a variety of roles during my four years of university training. I am able to adapt to different environments and put my skills and abilities to immediate use.

I am writing to you because your bank may be in need of an accomplished candidate with my years of experience, education, and training for your management trainee program. If so, you may be interested in some of my achievements:

- A position as a bank teller during a summer work-study program gave me a general understanding of bank functions.

- Promotion to New Accounts Counselor, advising customers on the various banking services we provided, allowed me to interact with customers and learn more about banking practices.

- An internship as an assistant loan officer, taking credit histories and analyzing credit risks, helped develop my analytical skills.

- As an assistant in the financial aid office at my university, I have developed excellent listening and organizational skills.

I received my B.A. in economics from the University of New Mexico in June 2000.

It would be a pleasure to review my qualifications with you in a personal interview. I will call your office at the end of next week to make arrangements for an interview if you are interested. Thank you for your consideration.

Sincerely,

Dan Conrad

make a number of potential employers aware of your availability and expertise. Because the broadcast letter is mass-mailed (five to six hundred employers), the amount of work required may not be worth the return. If you choose to mail out a broadcast letter, you can expect to receive a response from 2 to 5 percent, at best, of the organizations that receive your letter.

A broadcast letter is most often used by individuals who have an extensive and quantifiable work history. College students often do not have the credentials and work experience to support using a broadcast letter, and most will find it difficult to effectively quantify a slim work history.

A broadcast letter is generally four paragraphs (one page) long. The first paragraph should immediately gain the attention of the reader and state some unusual accomplishment or skill that would be of benefit to the organization. It also states the reason for the letter. Details of the sender's work history are revealed in the third paragraph. These can appear in paragraph form or as a bulleted list. Education and other qualifications or credentials are then described. Finally, the job seeker indicates what he or she will do to follow up on the letter, which usually is a follow-up call one to two weeks after the letter is sent.

RESUME PRODUCTION AND OTHER TIPS

If you have the option and convenience of using a laser printer, you may want to initially produce a limited number of copies of your resume in case you want or need to make changes.

Resume paper color should be carefully chosen. You should consider the types of employers who will receive your resume and the types of positions for which you are applying. Use white or ivory paper for traditional or conservative employers or for higher-level positions.

Black ink on sharply white paper can be harsh on the reader's eyes. Think about an ivory or cream paper that will provide less contrast and be easier to read. Pink, green, and blue tints should generally be avoided.

Many resume writers buy packages of matching envelopes and cover sheet stationery that, although not absolutely necessary, convey a professional impression.

If you'll be producing many cover letters at home, be sure you have high-quality printing equipment, whether it be computerized or standard typewriter equipment. Learn standard envelope formats for business and retain a copy of every cover letter you send out. You can use it to take notes of any telephone conversations that may occur.

If attending a job fair, women generally can fold their resume in thirds lengthwise and find it fits into a clutch bag or envelope-style purse. Both men and women will have no trouble if they carry a briefcase. For men without a briefcase, carry the resume in a nicely covered legal-size pad holder or fold it in half lengthwise and place it inside your suitcoat pocket, taking care it doesn't "float" outside your collar.

THE COVER LETTER

The cover letter provides you with the opportunity to tailor your resume by telling the prospective employer how you can be a benefit to the organization. It will allow you to highlight aspects of your background that are not already discussed in your resume and that might be especially relevant to the organization you are contacting or to the position you are seeking. Every resume should have a cover letter enclosed when you send it out. Unlike the resume, which may be mass-produced, a cover letter is most effective when it is individually typed and focused on the particular requirements of the organization in question.

A good cover letter should supplement the resume and motivate the reader to review the resume. The format shown in Exhibit 2.6 is only a suggestion to help you decide what information to include in writing a cover letter.

Exhibit 2.6

Cover Letter Format

Your Street Address
Your Town, State, Zip
Phone Number
E-mail

Date

Name
Title
Organization
Address

Dear _____:

First Paragraph. In this paragraph state the reason for the letter, name the specific position or type of work you are applying for, and indicate from which resource (career development office, newspaper, contact, employment service) you learned of the opening. The first paragraph can also be used to inquire about future openings.

Second Paragraph. Indicate why you are interested in the position, the company, its products or services, and what you can do for the employer. If you are a recent graduate, explain how your academic background makes you a qualified candidate. Try not to repeat the same information found in the resume.

Third Paragraph. Refer the reader to the enclosed resume for more detailed information.

Fourth Paragraph. In this paragraph say what you will do to follow up on your letter. For example, state that you will call by a certain

continued

---

continued

date to set up an interview or to find out if the company will be recruiting in your area. Finish by indicating your willingness to answer any questions they may have. Be sure you have provided your phone number.

Sincerely,

Type your name

Enclosure

Begin the cover letter with your street address twelve lines down from the top. Leave three to five lines between the date and the name of the person to whom you are addressing the cover letter. Make sure you leave one blank line between the salutation and the body of the letter and between paragraphs. After typing "Sincerely," leave four blank lines and type your name. This should leave plenty of room for your signature. A sample cover letter is shown in Exhibit 2.7.

The following guidelines will help you write good cover letters:

1. Be sure to type your letter; ensure there are no misspellings.

2. Avoid unusual typefaces, such as script.

3. Address the letter to an individual, using the person's name and title. To obtain this information, call the company. If answering a blind newspaper advertisement, address the letter "To Whom It May Concern" or omit the salutation.

4. Be sure your cover letter directly indicates the position you are applying for and tells why you are qualified to fill it.

5. Send the original letter, not a photocopy, with your resume. Keep a copy for your records.

6. Make your cover letter no more than one page.

7. Include a phone number where you can be reached.

8. Avoid trite language and have someone read it over to react to its tone, content, and mechanics.

9. For your own information, record the date you send out each letter and resume.

Exhibit 2.7

Sample Cover Letter

Jason Sherman
156 Winchester Street
Brookline, MA 02146
(617) 555-2470
jassher@aol.com

May 11, 2000

Anna Lopez
Director of Personnel
Polaroid Corporation
7568 Route 128
Waltham, MA 02178

Dear Ms. Lopez:

I read of your opening for an assistant contracts manager in the May 9, 2000, issue of *The Boston Globe,* and I am very interested in the possibilities it offers. The ad indicates that you are looking for a creative team player with good communication skills and human resources experience. I believe my background and skills match this description.

In June of 2000, I will graduate from Northeastern University with a bachelor of arts degree in economics and a minor in human resources. In addition to my economics and human resources course work, I have also completed a computer science class on the use of spreadsheets and databases.

As you can see on my resume, I have significant work experience in human resources. For three years, I worked in Northeastern's personnel department, in the benefits branch and then in contracts. This experience taught me a great deal about the personnel concerns of a major employer, including employee contracts, policy, and teamwork. I believe that this experience would translate well to a corporate setting.

continued

continued

I have heard good things about Polaroid and would appreciate the opportunity to meet with you to discuss the job opening. I will contact your office next week to follow up my letter and, if you are interested, to set up an interview. In the meantime, please call (617) 555-2470 or E-mail (jassher@aol.com) me if you have questions. Thank you for your consideration.

Sincerely,

Jason Sherman

Enclosure: resume

CHAPTER THREE

RESEARCHING CAREERS

∙∙∙

Many economics majors make their degree choice with the expectation that their degree will be the ticket to employment after graduation. But economics is a vast field, populated with hundreds of job titles, some you might not have heard of or thought of before. You know that an economics major has given you an overview of government systems, banking, finance, and other related subjects. However, you still may be confused about exactly what kinds of jobs you are qualified for with your degree and what kinds of organizations are likely to hire you. Are all of the economics-related jobs slated for master's degree or doctorate recipients? Where can an economics major fit into a hospital, insurance company, or law office?

∙∙∙

WHAT DO THEY CALL THE JOB YOU WANT?

There is every reason to be unaware. One reason for confusion is perhaps a mistaken assumption that a college education provides job training. In most cases it does not. Of course, applied fields such as engineering, management, or education provide specific skills for the workplace, whereas most liberal arts degrees simply provide an education. A liberal arts education exposes you to numerous fields of study and teaches you quantitative reasoning, critical thinking, writing, and speaking, all of which can be successfully applied to a number of different job fields. But it still remains up to you to choose a job field and to learn how to articulate the benefits of your education in a way the employer will appreciate.

As indicated in Chapter 1 on self-assessment, your first task is to understand and value what parts of that education you enjoyed and were good at and would continue to enjoy in your life's work. Did your writing courses encourage you in your ability to express yourself in writing? Did you enjoy the research process, and did you find your work was well received? Did you enjoy any of your required quantitative subjects like algebra or calculus?

The answers to questions such as these provide clues to skills and interests you bring to the employment market over and above the credential of your degree. In fact, it is not an overstatement to suggest that most employers who demand a college degree immediately look beyond that degree to you as a person and your own individual expression of what you like to do and think you can do for them, regardless of your major.

COLLECTING JOB TITLES

The world of employment is a big place, and even seasoned veterans of the job hunt can be surprised about what jobs are to be found in what organizations. You need to become a bit of an explorer and adventurer and be willing to try a variety of techniques to begin a list of possible occupations that might use your talents and education. Once you have a list of possibilities that you are interested in and qualified for, you can move on to find out what kinds of organizations have these job titles.

Not every employer seeking to hire an economist may be equally desirable to you. Some employment environments may be more attractive to you than others. An economics major considering government service, for example, could do that as a civil servant, a member of the armed forces, an elected representative, or a foreign service officer.

Each type of employment environment presents a different "culture" with associated norms in the pace of work, the subject matter of interest, and the backgrounds of its employees. Although the job titles may be the same, not all locations will present the same "fit" for you.

If you majored in economics and enjoyed the in-class presentations you did as part of your degree and have developed some strong communication skills, you might naturally think of public affairs within a government agency. But economics majors with these same skills and interests might go on to teach others their skills, or work in human resources, banking, or as an attorney, after completing law school.

••

Take training, for example. Trainers write policy and procedural manuals and actively assist all levels of employees in mastering various tasks and work-related systems. Trainers exist in all large corporations, banks, consumer goods manufacturers, medical diagnostic equipment firms, sales organizations, and any organization that has processes or materials that need to be presented to and learned by the staff.

In reading job descriptions or want ads for any of these positions, you would find your four-year degree a "must." However, the academic major might be less important than your own individual skills in critical thinking, analysis, report writing, public presentations, and interpersonal communication. Even more important than thinking or knowing you have certain skills is your ability to express those skills concretely and the examples you use to illustrate them to an employer.

The best beginning to a job search is to create a list of job titles you might want to pursue, learn more about the nature of the jobs behind those titles, and then discover what kinds of employers hire for those positions. In the following section we'll teach you how to build a job title directory to use in your job search.

Developing a Job Title Directory That Works for You

A job title directory is simply a complete list of all the job titles you are interested in, are intrigued by, or think you are qualified for. Combining the understanding gained through self-assessment with your own individual interests and the skills and talents you've acquired with your degree, you'll soon start to read and recognize a number of occupational titles that seem right for you. There are several resources you can use to develop your list, including computer searches, books, and want ads.

Computerized Interest Inventories. One way to begin your search is to identify a number of jobs that call for your degree and the particular skills and interests you identified as part of the self-assessment process. There are excellent interactive computer career guidance programs on the market to help you produce such selected lists of possible job titles. Most of these are available at high schools and colleges and at some larger town and city libraries. Two of the industry leaders are SIGI and DISCOVER. Both allow you to enter interests, values, educational background, and other information to produce lists of possible occupations and industries. Each of the resources listed here will produce different job title lists. Some job titles will appear again and again, while others will be unique to a particular source. Investigate them all!

Reference Books. Books on the market that may be available through your local library, bookstore, or career counseling office also suggest various occupations related to a number of majors. Two of the many good books on the market are *Occupational Outlook Handbook (OOH)* and *Occupational Projections and Training Data*, both put out annually by the U.S. Department of Labor, Bureau of Labor Statistics. The *OOH* describes hundreds of job titles under several broad categories, such as executive, administrative, and managerial occupations, and also identifies those jobs by their *Dictionary of Occupational Titles (DOT)* code. (See the following discussion.)

· ·

For economics majors, careers are listed throughout various sections of the *OOH*. If you were to look up *economist,* you would be directed to the section on economists and market research analysts. Information on life underwriters would be categorized under insurance agents and brokers. Education and training manager information would lead you to human resources specialists and managers. The *OOH* also provides information in these and other categories on job outlook and training requirements. Many additional job titles are provided in each section under "Related Occupations."

The *Occupational Projections and Training Data* is another good resource that essentially allows job seekers to compare five hundred occupations on factors such as

job openings, earnings, and training requirements. So, if as an economics major you discover market researcher as a job title in the *OOH*, you can then go to the *Occupational Projections and Training Data* and compare it with scores of jobs related to that title. This source adds some depth by presenting statistics in a number of different occupations within that field.

....

Each job title deserves your consideration. Like the layers of an onion, the search for job titles can go on and on! As you spend time doing this activity, you are actually learning more about the value of your degree. What's important in your search at this point is not to become critical or selective, but rather to develop as long a list of possibilities as you can. Every source used will help you add new and potentially exciting jobs to your growing list.

Want Ads. It has been well publicized that newspaper want ads represent only about 10 to 15 percent of the current job market. Nevertheless, the Sunday want ads can be a great help to you in your search. Although they may not be the best place to look for a job, they can teach the job seeker much about the job market and provide a good education in job descriptions, duties and responsibilities, active industries, and some indication of the volume of job traffic. For our purposes they are a good source for job titles to add to your list.

Read the Sunday want ads in a major market newspaper for several Sundays in a row. Circle and then cut out any and all ads that interest you and seem to call for something close to your education and experience. Remember, because want ads are written for what an organization *hopes* to find, you don't have to meet absolutely every criterion. However, if certain requirements are stated as absolute minimums and you cannot meet them, it's best not to waste your time.

A recent examination of *The Boston Sunday Globe* revealed the following possible occupations for a liberal arts major with some computer skills and limited prior work experience. (This is only a partial list of what was available.)

- Admissions representative
- Salesperson
- Compliance director
- Technical writer
- Personnel trainee
- GED examiner

- Assistant principal gifts writer
- Public relations officer
- Direct mail researcher
- Associate publicist

After performing this exercise for a few Sundays, you'll find you have collected a new library of job titles.

The Sunday want ad exercise is important because these jobs are out in the marketplace. They truly exist, and people with your qualifications are being sought to apply. What's more, many of these advertisements describe the duties and responsibilities of the job advertised and give you a beginning sense of the challenges and opportunities such a position presents. Some will indicate salary, and that will be helpful as well. This information will better define the jobs for you and provide some good material for possible interviews in that field.

Exploring Job Descriptions

Once you've arrived at a solid list of possible job titles that interest you and for which you believe you are somewhat qualified, it's a good idea to do some research on each of these jobs. The preeminent source for such job information is the *Dictionary of Occupational Titles* or *DOT*. This directory lists every conceivable job and provides excellent up-to-date information on duties and responsibilities, interactions with associates, and day-to-day assignments and tasks. These descriptions provide a thorough job analysis, but they do not consider the possible employers or the environments in which a job may be performed. So, although a position as public relations officer may be well defined in terms of duties and responsibilities, it does not explain the differences in doing public relations work in a college or a hospital or a factory or a bank. You will need to look somewhere else for information about work settings.

Learning More About Possible Work Settings

After reading some job descriptions, you may choose to edit and revise your list of job titles once again, discarding those you feel are not suitable and keeping those that continue to hold your interest. Or you may wish to keep your list intact and see where these jobs may be located. For example, if you are interested in public relations and you appear to have those skills and the requisite education, you'll want to know what organizations do public relations. How can you find that out? How much income does someone in public relations make a year, and what is the employment potential for the field of public relations?

To answer these and many other good questions about your list of job titles, we recommend you try any of the following resources: *Careers*

Encyclopedia, Career Information Center, College to Career: The Guide to Job Opportunities, and the *Occupational Outlook Handbook.* Each of these books, in a different way, will help to put the job titles you have selected into an employer context. *VGM's Handbook of Business and Management Careers* contains detailed career descriptions for more than fifty fields. Entries include complete information on duties and responsibilities for individual careers and detailed entry-level requirements. There is information on working conditions and promotional opportunities as well. Salary ranges and career outlook projections are also provided. Perhaps the most extensive discussion is found in the *Occupational Outlook Handbook,* which gives a thorough presentation of the nature of the work, the working conditions, employment statistics, training, other qualifications, and advancement possibilities as well as job outlook and earnings. Related occupations are also detailed, and a select bibliography is provided to help you find additional information.

Continuing with our public relations example, your search through these reference materials would teach you that the public relations jobs you find attractive are available in larger hospitals, financial institutions, most corporations (both consumer goods and industrial goods), media organizations, and colleges and universities.

Networking to Get the Complete Story

You now have not only a list of job titles but also, for each of these job titles, a description of the work involved and a general list of possible employment settings in which to work. You'll want to do some reading and keep talking to friends, colleagues, teachers, and others about the possibilities. Don't neglect to ask if the career office at your college maintains some kind of alumni network. Often such alumni networks will connect you with another graduate from the college who is working in the job title or industry you are seeking information about. These career networkers offer what assistance they can. For some it is a full day "shadowing" the alumnus as he or she goes about the job. Others offer partial-day visits, tours, informational interviews, resume reviews, job postings, or, if distance prevents a visit, telephone interviews. As fellow graduates, they'll be frank and informative about their own jobs and prospects in their field.

Take them up on their offer and continue to learn all you can about your own personal list of job titles, descriptions, and employment settings. You'll probably continue to edit and refine this list as you learn more about the realities of the job, the possible salary, advancement opportunities, and supply and demand statistics.

In the next section we'll describe how to find the specific organizations that represent these industries and employers so that you can begin to make contact.

WHERE ARE THESE JOBS, ANYWAY?

Having a list of job titles that you've designed around your own career interests and skills is an excellent beginning. It means you've really thought about who you are and what you are presenting to the employment market. It has caused you to think seriously about the most appealing environments to work in, and you have identified some employer types that represent these environments.

The research and the thinking that you've done thus far will be used again and again. They will be helpful in writing your resume and cover letters, in talking about yourself on the telephone to prospective employers, and in answering interview questions.

Now is a good time to begin to narrow the field of job titles and employment sites down to some specific employers to initiate the employment contact.

Finding Out Which Employers Hire People Like You

This section will provide tips, techniques, and specific resources for developing an actual list of specific employers that can be used to make contacts. It is an outline that you must be prepared to tailor to your own particular needs and according to what you bring to the job search. Once again, it is important to stress the need to communicate with others along the way exactly what you're looking for and what your goals are for the research you're doing. Librarians, employers, career counselors, friends, friends of friends, business contacts, and bookstore staff will all have helpful information on geographically specific and new resources to aid you in locating employers who'll hire you.

Identifying Information Resources

Your interview wardrobe and your new resume may have put a dent in your wallet, but the resources you'll need to pursue your job search are available for free (although you might choose to copy materials on a machine instead of taking notes by hand). The categories of information detailed here are not hard to find and are yours for the browsing.

Numerous resources described in this section will help you identify actual employers. Use all of them or any others that you identify as available in your geographic area. As you become experienced in this process, you'll quickly figure out which information sources are helpful and which are not. If you live in a rural area, a well-planned day trip to a major city that includes a college career office, a large college or city library, state and federal employment centers, a chamber of commerce office, and a well-stocked bookstore can produce valuable results.

There are many excellent resources available to help you identify actual job sites. They are categorized into employer directories (usually indexed by product lines and geographic location), geographically based directories (designed to highlight particular cities, regions, or states), career-specific directories (e.g., *Sports Market Place,* which lists tens of thousands of firms involved with sports), periodicals and newspapers, targeted job posting publications, and videos. This is by no means meant to be a complete list of resources but rather a starting point for identifying useful resources.

Working from the more general references to highly specific resources, we provide a basic list to help you begin your search. Many of these you'll find easily available. In some cases, reference librarians and others will suggest even better materials for your particular situation. Start to create your own customized bibliography of job-search references. Use copying services to save time and to allow you to carry away information about organizations' missions, locations, officers, phone numbers, and addresses.

Employer Directories. There are many employer directories available to give you the kind of information you need for your job search. Some of our favorites are listed here, but be sure to ask the professionals you are working with to make additional suggestions.

- *America's Corporate Families* identifies many major U.S. ultimate parent companies and displays corporate family linkage of subsidiaries and divisions. Businesses can be identified by their industrial code.

- *Million Dollar Directory: America's Leading Public and Private Companies* lists about 160,000 companies.

- *Moody's* various manuals are intended as guides for investors, so they contain a history of each company. Each manual contains a classification of companies by industries and products.

- *Standard and Poor's Register of Corporations* contains listings for 45,000 businesses, some of which are not listed in the *Million Dollar Directory.*

- *Job Seekers Guide to Private and Public Companies* profiles 15,000 employers in four volumes, each covering a different geographic region. Company entries include contact information, business descriptions, and application procedures.

- *The Career Guide: Dun's Employment Opportunities Directory* lists more than 5,000 large organizations, including hospitals and local governments. Profiles include an overview and history of the employer as well as opportunities, benefits, and contact names. It contains geographic and industrial indexes and indexes by discipline or internship availability. This guide also includes a state-by-state list of professional personnel consultants and their specialties.

❑ *Professional's Job Finder/Government Job Finder/Non-Profits Job Finder* are specific directories of job services, salary surveys, and periodical listings in which you can find advertisements for jobs in the professional, government, or nonprofit sector.

❑ *Opportunities in Nonprofit Organizations* is a VGM career series edition that opens up the world of nonprofit organizations by helping you match your interest profile to the aims and objectives of scores of nonprofit employers in business, education, health and medicine, social welfare, science and technology, and so on. There is also a special section on fund-raising and development career paths.

❑ *The 100 Best Companies to Sell For* lists companies by industry, provides contact information, and describes benefits and corporate culture.

❑ *The 100 Best Companies to Work for in America* rates organizations on several factors including opportunities, job security, and pay.

❑ *Companies That Care* lists organizations that the authors believe are family-friendly. One index organizes information by state.

❑ *Infotrac CD-ROM Business Index* covers business journals and magazines and can provide information on public and private companies.

❑ *ABI/Inform on Disc* (CD-ROM) indexes articles in more than eight hundred journals.

Geographically Based Directories. The Job Bank series published by Bob Adams, Inc., contains detailed entries on each area's major employers, including business activity, address, phone number, and hiring contact name. Many listings specify educational backgrounds being sought in potential employees. Each volume contains a solid discussion of each city's or state's major employment sectors. Organizations are also indexed by industry. Job Bank volumes are available for the following places: Atlanta, Boston, Chicago, Denver, Dallas–Ft. Worth, Florida, Houston, Ohio, St. Louis, San Francisco, Seattle, Los Angeles, New York, Detroit, Philadelphia, Minneapolis, the Northwest, and Washington, D.C.

National Job Bank lists employers in every state, along with contact names and commonly hired job categories. Included are many small companies often overlooked by other directories. Companies are also indexed by industry. This publication provides information on educational backgrounds sought and lists company benefits.

Career-Specific Directories. VGM publishes a number of excellent series detailing careers for college graduates. In the Professional Careers series are guides to careers in the following fields, among others:

- Advertising
- Business
- Communications
- Computers
- Health Care
- High Tech

Each provides an excellent discussion of the industry, educational requirements for jobs, salary ranges, duties, and projected outlooks for the field.

Another VGM series, Opportunities in . . . , has an equally wide range of titles relating to specific majors, such as the following:

- *Opportunities in Banking*
- *Opportunities in Insurance*
- *Opportunities in Film*
- *Opportunities in Music*
- *Opportunities in Journalism*
- *Opportunities in Law*
- *Opportunities in Government*
- *Opportunities in Teaching*
- *Opportunities in Nursing*

Periodicals and Newspapers. Several sources are available to help you locate which journals or magazines carry job advertisements in your field. Other resources help you identify opportunities in other parts of the country.

❑ *Where the Jobs Are: A Comprehensive Directory of 1,200 Journals Listing Career Opportunities* links specific occupational titles to corresponding periodicals that carry job listings for your field.

❑ *Social & Behavioral Sciences Jobs Handbook* contains a periodicals matrix organized by academic discipline and highlights periodicals containing job listings.

❑ *National Business Employment Weekly* compiles want ads from four regional editions of the *Wall Street Journal.* Most are business and management positions.

❑ *National Ad Search* reprints ads from seventy-five metropolitan newspapers across the country. Although the focus is on management positions, technical and professional postings are also included. *Caution:* Watch deadline dates carefully on listings because deadlines may have already passed by the time the ad is printed.

❑ *The Federal Jobs Digest* and *Federal Career Opportunities* list government positions.

❑ *World Chamber of Commerce Directory* lists addresses for chambers worldwide, state boards of tourism, convention and visitors' bureaus, and economic development organizations.

This list is certainly not exhaustive; use it to begin your job search work.

Targeted Job Posting Publications. Although the resources that follow are national in scope, they are either targeted to one medium of contact (telephone), focused on specific types of jobs, or are less comprehensive than the sources previously listed.

❑ *Job Hotlines USA* pinpoints more than one thousand hard-to-find telephone numbers for companies and government agencies that use prerecorded job messages and listings. Very few of the telephone numbers listed are toll-free, and sometimes recordings are long, so callers beware!

❑ *The Job Hunter* is a national biweekly newspaper listing business, arts, media, government, human services, health, community-related, and student services job openings.

❑ *Current Jobs for Graduates* is a national employment listing for liberal arts professions, including editorial positions, management opportunities, museum work, teaching, and nonprofit work.

❑ *Environmental Opportunities* serves environmental job interests nationwide by listing administrative, marketing, and human resources positions along with education-related jobs and positions directly related to a degree in an environmental field.

❑ *Y National Vacancy List* shows YMCA professional vacancies, including development, administration, programming, membership, and recreation postings.

❑ *ARTSearch* is a national employment service bulletin for the arts, including administration, managerial, marketing, and financial management jobs.

❑ *Community Jobs* is an employment newspaper for the nonprofit sector that provides a variety of listings, including project manager, canvas director, government relations specialist, community organizer, and program instructor.

❑ *College Placement Council Annual: A Guide to Employment Opportunities for College Graduates* is an annual guide containing solid job-hunting information and, more importantly, displaying ads from large corporations actively seeking recent college graduates in all majors. Company profiles provide brief descriptions and available employment opportunities. Contact names and addresses are given. Profiles are indexed by organization name, geographic location, and occupation.

Videos. You may be one of the many job seekers who like to get information via a medium other than paper. Many career libraries, public libraries, and career centers in libraries carry an assortment of videos that will help you learn new techniques and get information helpful in the job search. A small sampling of the multitude of videos now available includes the following:

❑ *The Skills Search* (20 min.) discusses three types of skills important in the workplace, how to present the skills in an interview, and how to respond to problem questions.

❑ *Effective Answers to Interview Questions* (35 min.) presents two real-life job seekers and shows how they realized the true meaning of interview questions and formulated positive answers.

❑ *Employer's Expectations* (33 min.) covers three areas that are important to all employers: appearance, dependability, and skills.

❑ *The Tough New Labor Market of the 1990s* (30 min.) presents labor market facts as well as suggestions on what job seekers should do to gain employment in this market.

❑ *Dialing for Jobs: Using the Phone in the Job Search* (30 min.) describes how to use the phone effectively to gain information and arrange interviews by following two new graduates as they learn and apply techniques.

Locating Information Resources

An essay by John Case that appeared in the *Boston Globe* alerts both new and seasoned job seekers that the job market is changing, and the old guarantees of lifelong employment no longer hold true. Some of our major corporations, which were once seen as the most prestigious of employment destinations, are now laying off thousands of employees. Middle management is especially hard hit in downsizing situations. On the other side of the coin, smaller, more entrepreneurial firms are adding employees and realizing enormous profit margins. The geography of the new job market is unfamiliar, and the terrain is much harder to map. New and smaller firms can mean different kinds of jobs and new job titles. The successful job seeker will keep an open mind about where he or she might find employment and what that employment might be called.

In order to become familiar with this new terrain, you will need to undertake some research, which can be done at any of the following locations:

❑ Public libraries

❑ Business organizations

❑ Employment agencies

❑ Bookstores

❑ Career libraries

Each one of these places offers a collection of resources that will help you get the information you need.

As you meet and talk with service professionals at all these sites, be sure to let them know what you're doing. Inform them of your job search, what you've already accomplished, and what you're looking for. The more people who know you're job seeking, the greater the possibility that someone will have information or know someone who can help you along your way.

Public Libraries. Large city libraries, college and university libraries, and even well-supported town library collections contain a variety of resources to help you conduct a job search. It is not uncommon for libraries to have separate "vocational choices" sections with books, tapes, and associated materials relating to job search and selection. Some are now even making resume creation software available for use by patrons.

Some of the publications we name throughout this book are expensive reference items that are rarely purchased by individuals. In addition, libraries carry a wide range of newspapers and telephone yellow pages as well as the usual array of books. If resources are not immediately available, many libraries have loan arrangements with other facilities and can make information available to you relatively quickly.

Take advantage of not only the reference collections, but also the skilled and informed staff. Let them know exactly what you are looking for, and they'll have their own suggestions. You'll be visiting the library frequently, and the reference staff will soon come to know who you are and what you're working on. They'll be part of your job search network!

Business Organizations. Chambers of commerce, offices of new business development, councils on business and industry, Small Business Administration (SBA) offices, and professional associations can all provide geographically specific lists of companies and organizations that have hiring needs. They also have an array of other available materials, including visitors' guides and regional fact books that provide additional employment information.

These agencies serve to promote local and regional businesses and ensure their survival and success. Although these business organizations do not advertise job openings or seek employees for their members, they may be very aware of staffing needs among their member firms. In your visits to each of these locations, spend some time with the personnel, getting to know who they are and what they do. Let them know of your job search and your intentions regarding employment. You may be surprised and delighted at the information they may provide.

Employment Agencies. Employment agencies (including state and federal employment offices), professional "headhunters" or executive search firms, and some private career counselors can provide direct leads to job openings. Don't overlook these resources. If you are mounting a complete job search program and want to ensure that you are covering the potential market for employers, consider the employment agencies in your territory. Some of these organizations work contractually with several specific firms and may have access that is unavailable to you. Others may be particularly well-informed about supply and demand in particular industries or geographic locations.

In the case of professional (commercial) employment agencies, which include those executive recruitment firms labeled "headhunters," you should be cautious about entering into any binding contractual agreement. Before doing so, be sure to get the information you need to decide whether their services can be of use to you. Questions to ask include the following: Who pays the fee when employment is obtained? Are there any other fees or costs associated with this service? What is their placement rate? Can you see a list of previous clients and can you talk to any for references? Do they typically work with entry-level job seekers? Do they tend to focus on particular kinds of employment or industries?

A few cautions are in order, however, when you work with professional agencies. Remember, the professional employment agency is, in most cases, paid by the hiring organization. Naturally, their interest and attention is largely directed to the employer, not to the candidate. Of course, they want to provide good candidates to guarantee future contracts, but they are less interested in the job seeker than the employer.

For teacher candidates, there are a number of good placement firms that charge the prospective teacher, not the employer. This situation has evolved over time as a result of supply and demand and financial structuring of most school systems, which cannot spend money on recruiting teachers. Usually these firms charge a nonrefundable administrative fee and, upon successful placement, require a fee based on percentage of salary, which may range from 10 to 20 percent of annual compensation. Often, this can be paid over a number of months. Check your contract carefully.

State and federal employment offices are no-fee services that maintain extensive "job boards" and can provide detailed specifications for each job advertised and help with application forms. Because government employment application forms are detailed, keep a master copy along with copies of all additional documentation (resumes, educational transcripts, military discharge papers, proof of citizenship, etc.). Successive applications may require separate filings. Visit these offices as frequently as you can because most deal with applicants on a "walk-in" basis and will not telephone prospective candidates or maintain files of job seekers. Check your telephone book for the address of the nearest state and federal offices.

One type of employment service that causes much confusion among job seekers is the outplacement firm. Their advertisements tend to suggest they will put you in touch with the "hidden job market." They use advertising phrases such as "We'll work with you until you get that job" or "Maximize your earnings and career opportunities." In fact, if you read the fine print on these ads, you will notice these firms must state they are "Not an employment agency." These firms are, in fact, corporate and private outplacement counseling agencies whose work involves resume editing, counseling on how to obtain job leads, interview skills training, and all the other aspects of hiring preparation. They do this for a fee, sometimes in the thousands of dollars range, which is paid by you, the client. Some of these firms have good reputations and provide excellent materials and techniques. Most, however, provide a service you as a college student or graduate can receive free from your alma mater or through a reciprocity agreement between your college and a college or university located closer to your current address.

Bookstores. Any well-stocked bookstore will carry some job search books that are worth buying. Some major stores will even have an extensive section devoted to materials, including excellent videos, related to the job search process. You will also find copies of local newspapers and business magazines. The one advantage that is provided by resources purchased at a bookstore is that you can read and work with the information in the comfort of your own home and do not have to conform to the hours of operation of a library, which can present real difficulties if you are working full time as you seek employment. A few minutes spent browsing in a bookstore might be a beneficial break from your job search activities and turn up valuable resources.

Career Libraries. Career libraries, which are found in career centers at colleges and universities and sometimes within large public libraries, contain a unique blend of the job search resources housed in other settings. In addition, career libraries often purchase a number of job listing publications, each of which targets a specific industry or type of job. You may find job listings specifically for entry-level positions for economics majors. Ask about job posting newsletters or newspapers specifically focused on careers in the area that most interests you. Each center will be unique, but you are certain to discover some good sources of jobs.

Most college career libraries now hold growing collections of video material on specific industries and on aspects of your job search process, including dress and appearance, how to manage the luncheon or dinner interview, how to be effective at a job fair, and many other specific titles. Some larger corporations produce handsome video materials detailing the variety of career paths and opportunities available in their organizations.

Some career libraries also house computer-based career planning and information systems. These interactive computer programs help you to clarify your values and interests and will combine that with your education to provide possible job titles and industry locations. Some even contain extensive lists of graduate school programs.

A career library also will be able to direct you to computerized job search services. These services, of which there are many, are run by private companies, individual colleges, or consortiums of colleges. They attempt to match qualified job candidates with potential employers. The candidate submits a resume (or an application) to the service. This information (which can be categorized into hundreds of separate "fields" of data) is entered into a computer database. Your information is then compared with the information from employers about what they desire in a prospective employee. If there is a match between what they want and what you have indicated you can offer, the job search service or the employer will contact you directly to continue the process.

Computerized job search services can complement an otherwise complete job search program. They are *not*, however, a substitute for the kinds of activities described in this book. They are essentially passive operations that are random in nature. If you have not listed skills, abilities, traits, experiences, or education *exactly* as an employer has listed its needs, there is simply no match.

Consult with the staff members at the career libraries you use. These professionals have been specifically trained to meet the unique needs you present. Often you can just drop in and receive help with general questions, or you may want to set up an appointment to speak one-on-one with a career counselor to gain special assistance.

Every career library is different in size and content, but each can provide valuable information for the job search. Some may even provide some limited counseling. If you have not visited the career library at your college or alma mater, call and ask if these collections are still available for your use. Be sure to ask about other services that you can use as well.

If you are not near your own college as you work on your job search, call the career office and inquire about reciprocal agreements with other colleges that are closer to where you live. Very often your own alma mater can arrange for you to use a limited menu of services at another school. This typically would include access to a career library and job posting information and might include limited counseling.

CHAPTER FOUR

NETWORKING

Networking is the process of deliberately establishing relationships to get career-related information or to alert potential employers that you are available for work. Networking is critically important to today's job seeker for two reasons: it will help you get the information you need, and it can help you find out about *all* of the available jobs.

Getting the Information You Need

Networkers will review your resume and give you candid feedback on its effectiveness. They will talk about the job you are looking for and give you a candid appraisal of how they see your strengths and weaknesses. If they have a good sense of the industry or the employment sector for that job, you'll get their feelings on future trends in the industry as well. Some networkers will be very candid about salaries, job hunting techniques, and suggestions for your job search strategy. Many have been known to place calls right from the interview desk to friends and associates who might be interested in you. Each networker will make his or her own contribution, and each will be valuable.

Because organizations must evolve to adapt to current global market needs, the information provided by decision makers within various organizations will be critical to your success as a new job market entrant. Networking can help you find out about trends currently affecting the industries under your consideration.

Finding Out About All of the Available Jobs

Not every job that is available at this very moment is advertised for potential applicants to see. This is called the *hidden job market.* Only 15 to 20 percent of all jobs are formally advertised, which means that 80 to 85 percent of available jobs do not appear in published channels. Networking will help you become more knowledgeable about all the employment opportunities available during your job search period.

Although someone you might talk to today doesn't know of any openings within his or her organization, tomorrow or next week or next month an opening may occur. If you've taken the time to show an interest in and knowledge of the organization, and if you've shown the company representative how you can help achieve organizational goals and that you can fit into the organization, you'll be one of the first candidates considered for the position.

Networking: A Proactive Approach

Networking is a proactive rather than a reactive approach. You, as a job seeker, are expected to initiate a certain level of activity on your own behalf; you cannot afford to simply respond to jobs listed in the newspaper. Being proactive means building a network of contacts that includes informed and interested decision makers who will provide you with up-to-date knowledge of the current job market and increase your chances of finding out about employment opportunities appropriate for your interests, experience, and level of education.

An old axiom of networking says, "You are only two phone calls away from the information you need." In other words, by talking to enough people, you will quickly come across someone who can offer you help. Start with your professors. Each of them probably has a wide circle of contacts. In their work and travel, they might have met someone who can help you or direct you to someone who can.

Control and the Networking Process

In deliberately establishing relationships, the process of networking begins with you in control—*you* are contacting specific individuals. As your network expands and you establish a set of professional relationships, your search for information or jobs will begin to move outside of your total control. A part of the networking process involves others assisting you by gathering information for you or recommending you as a possible job candidate. As additional people become a part of your networking system, you will have less knowledge about activities undertaken on your behalf; you will undoubtedly be contacted by individuals whom you did not initially approach. If you want to function effectively in surprise situations, you must be prepared at all times to talk with strangers about the informational or employment needs that motivated you to become involved in the networking process.

PREPARING TO NETWORK

In deliberately establishing relationships, maximize your efforts by organizing your approach. Five specific areas in which you can organize your efforts include reviewing your self-assessment, reviewing your research on job sites and organizations, deciding who it is you want to talk to, keeping track of all your efforts, and creating your self-promotion tools.

Review Your Self-Assessment

Your self-assessment is as important a tool in preparing to network as it has been in other aspects of your job search. You have carefully evaluated your personal traits, personal values, economic needs, longer-term goals, skill base, preferred skills, and underdeveloped skills. During the networking process, you will be called upon to communicate what you know about yourself and relate it to the information or job you seek. Be sure to review the exercises that you completed in the self-assessment section of this book in preparation for networking. We've explained that you need to assess what skills you have acquired from your major that are of general value to an employer and be ready to express those in ways employers can appreciate as useful in their own organizations.

Review Researching Job Sites and Organizations

In addition, individuals assisting you will expect that you'll have at least some background information on the occupation or industry of interest to you. Refer to the appropriate sections of this book and other relevant publications to acquire the background information necessary for effective networking. They'll explain how to identify not only the job titles that might be of interest to you, but also what kinds of organizations employ people to do that job. You will develop some sense of working conditions and expectations about duties and responsibilities—all of which will be of help in your networking interviews.

Decide Who It Is You Want to Talk To

Networking cannot begin until you decide who it is that you want to talk to and, in general, what type of information you hope to gain from your contacts. Once you know this, it's time to begin developing a list of contacts. Five useful sources for locating contacts are described here.

College Alumni Network. Most colleges and universities have created a formal network of alumni and friends of the institution who are particularly interested in helping currently enrolled students and graduates of their alma mater gain employment-related information.

••

Because economics is such a flexible degree program, you'll find an abundance of economics graduates spanning the full spectrum of possible employment. Just the diversity alone evidenced by such an alumni list should be encouraging and informative to the graduate. Among such a diversified group, there are likely to be many people you would enjoy talking with and perhaps could meet.

••

It is usually a simple process to make use of an alumni network. You need only visit the alumni or career office at your college or university and follow the procedure that has been established. Often, you will simply complete a form indicating your career goals and interests and you will be given the names of appropriate individuals to contact. In many cases staff members will coach you on how to make the best use of the limited time these alumni contacts may have available for you.

Alumni networkers may provide some combination of the following services: daylong shadowing experiences, telephone interviews, in-person interviews, information on relocating to given geographic areas, internship information, suggestions on graduate school study, and job vacancy notices.

••

What a valuable experience! Perhaps you are interested in a nonprofit administrative position but are concerned about your degree preparation and whether your capabilities are up to the requirements of the particular firm. Spending a day with an alumnus who works for a similar enterprise, asking lots of questions about his or her educational training and preparation, will give you a more concrete view of the possibilities for your degree. Observing firsthand how this person does the job will be a far better decision criterion for you than any reading on the subject could possibly be.

In addition to your own observations, the alumnus will have his or her own perspective on the relevance of

your training and will give you realistic and honest feedback on your job search concerns.

....

Present and Former Supervisors. If you believe you are on good terms with present or former job supervisors, they may be an excellent resource for providing information or directing you to appropriate resources that would have information related to your current interests and needs. Additionally, these supervisors probably belong to professional organizations, which they might be willing to utilize to get information for you.

....

If, for example, you were interested in working as a legislative assistant for a member of your state legislature, and you are currently working as a program director at the local chamber of commerce, talk with your supervisor or the executive director. He or she will probably know at least one state delegate or senator or influential members of the chamber who have strong political contacts. At least one of these people will probably be able to provide you with names and business telephone numbers of not only legislators, but also current staff members. You could then begin the networking process.

....

Employers in Your Area. Although you may be interested in working in a geographic location different from the one where you currently reside, don't overlook the value of the knowledge and contacts those around you are able to provide. Use the local telephone directory and newspaper to identify the types of organizations you are thinking of working for or professionals who have the kinds of jobs you are interested in. Recently, a call made to a local hospital's financial administrator for information on working in health care financial administration yielded more pertinent information on training seminars, regional professional organizations, and potential employment sites than a national organization was willing to provide.

Employers in Geographic Areas Where You Hope to Work. If you are thinking about relocating, identifying prospective employers or informational contacts in this new location will be critical to your success. Many resources are available to help you locate contact names. These include the yellow pages directory, the local newspapers, local or state business publications, and local chambers of commerce.

Professional Associations and Organizations. Professional associations and organizations can provide valuable information in several areas: career paths that you may not have considered, qualifications relating to those career choices, publications that list current job openings, and workshops or seminars that will enhance your professional knowledge and skills. They can also be excellent sources for background information on given industries: their health, current problems, and future challenges.

There are several excellent resources available to help you locate professional associations and organizations that would have information to meet your needs. Two especially useful publications are the *Encyclopedia of Associations* and the *National Trade and Professional Associations of the United States.*

Keep Track of All Your Efforts

It can be difficult, almost impossible, to remember all the details related to each contact you make during the networking process, so you will want to develop a record-keeping system that works for you. Formalize this process by using a computer database or a notebook or index cards to organize the information you gather. Begin by creating a list of the people or organizations you want to contact. Record the contact's name, address, telephone number, and what information you hope to gain. Each entry might look something like this:

Contact Name	Address	Phone #	Purpose
Mr. Tim Keefe	Wrigley Bldg.		
Dir. of Mines	Suite 72	(312) 555-8906	Resume screen

Once you have created this initial list, it will be helpful to keep more detailed information as you begin to actually make the contacts. Using the Network Contact Record form in Exhibit 4.1, keep good information on all your network contacts. They'll appreciate your recall of details of your meetings and conversations, and the information will help you to focus your networking efforts.

Exhibit 4.1

Network Contact Record

Name: Be certain your spelling is absolutely correct.

Title: Pick up a business card to be certain of the correct title.

Employing organization: Note any parent company or subsidiaries.

Business mailing address: This is often different from the street address.

Business telephone number: Include area code/alternative numbers/fax/E-mail.

Source for this contact: Who referred you, and what is their relationship?

Date of call or letter: Use plenty of space here to record multiple phone calls or visits, other employees you may have met, names of secretaries/ receptionists, etc.

Content of discussion: Keep enough notes here to remind you of the substance of your visits and telephone conversations in case some time elapses between contacts.

Follow-up necessary to continue working with this contact: Your contact may request that you send him or her some materials or direct you to contact an associate. Note any such instructions or assignments in this space.

Name of additional networker: Here you would record the
Address: names and phone numbers of
Phone: additional contacts met at this
Name of additional networker: employer's site. Often you will
Address: be introduced to many people,
Phone: some of whom may indicate
Name of additional networker: a willingness to help in your
Address: job search.
Phone:

Date thank-you note written: May help to date your next contact.

Follow-up action taken: Phone calls, visits, additional notes.

continued

---

continued

Other miscellaneous notes: Record any other additional interaction you think may be important to remember in working with this networking client. You will want this form in front of you when telephoning or just before and after a visit.

Create Your Self-Promotion Tools

There are two types of promotional tools that are used in the networking process. The first is a resume and cover letter, and the second is a one-minute "infomercial," which may be given over the telephone or in person.

Techniques for writing an effective resume and cover letter are covered in Chapter 2. Once you have reviewed that material and prepared these important documents, you will have created one of your self-promotion tools.

The one-minute infomercial will demand that you begin tying your interests, abilities, and skills to the people or organizations you want to network with. Think about your goal for making the contact to help you understand what you should say about yourself. You should be able to express yourself easily and convincingly. If, for example, you are contacting an alumnus of your institution to obtain the names of possible employment sites in a distant city, be prepared to discuss why you are interested in moving to that location, the types of jobs you are interested in, and the skills and abilities you possess that will make you a qualified candidate.

To create a meaningful one-minute infomercial, write it out, practice it if it will be a spoken presentation, rewrite it, and practice it again if necessary until expressing yourself comes easily and is convincing.

Here's a simplified example of an infomercial for use over the telephone:

••••••••••••••••••••••••••••••••••••

"Hello, Ms. Hamilton? My name is Joan Sanders. I am a recent graduate of State College, and I wish to enter the human resources field. I was an economics major and feel confident I have many of the skills I understand are valued in human resources, such as analytical and research skills, computer skills, and public speaking ability. What's more, I work well under pressure. I have read that can be a real advantage in this industry!

"Ms. Hamilton, I'm calling you because I still need more information about the human resources field and particularly how economics majors can contribute. I'm hoping you'll have the time to sit down with me for about half an hour and discuss your perspective on human resources careers. There are so many possible places to get into this field, and I am seeking some advice about which of those settings might be the best fit for my particular combination of skills and experience.

"Would you be willing to do that for me? I would greatly appreciate it. I am available most mornings, if that's convenient for you."

....

Other effective self-promotion tools include portfolios for those in the arts, writing professions, or teaching. Portfolios show examples of work, photographs of projects or classroom activities, or certificates and credentials that are job related. There may not be an opportunity to use the portfolio during an interview, and it is not something that should be left with the organization. It is designed to be explained and displayed by the creator. However, during some networking meetings, there may be an opportunity to illustrate a point or strengthen a qualification by exhibiting the portfolio.

BEGINNING THE NETWORKING PROCESS

Set the Tone for Your Contacts

It can be useful to establish "tone words" for any communications you embark upon. Before making your first telephone call or writing your first letter, decide what you want your contact to think of you. If you are networking to try to obtain a job, your tone words might include *genuine, informed,* and *self-knowledgeable.* When trying to acquire information, your tone words may have a slightly different focus, such as *courteous, organized, focused,* and *well-spoken.* Use the tone words you establish for your contacts to guide you through the networking process.

Honestly Express Your Intentions

When contacting individuals, it is important to be honest about your reasons for making the contact. Establish your purpose in your own mind and be able and ready to articulate it concisely. Determine an initial agenda, whether it be informational questioning or self-promotion, present it to your contact, and be ready to respond immediately. If you don't adequately prepare before initiating your contacts, you may find yourself at a disadvantage if you're asked to immediately begin your informational interview or self-promotion during the first phone conversation or visit.

Start Networking Within Your Circle of Confidence

Once you have organized your approach—by utilizing specific researching methods, creating a system for keeping track of the people you will contact, and developing effective self-promotion tools—you are ready to begin networking. The best place to begin networking is by talking with a group of people you trust and feel comfortable with. This group is usually made up of your family, friends, and career counselors. No matter who is in this inner circle, they will have a special interest in seeing you succeed in your job search. In addition, because they will be easy to talk to, you should try taking some risks in terms of practicing your information-seeking approach. Gain confidence in talking about the strengths you bring to an organization and the underdeveloped skills you feel hinder your candidacy. Be sure to review the section on self-assessment for tips on approaching each of these areas. Ask for critical but constructive feedback from the people in your circle of confidence on the letters you write and the one-minute infomercial you have developed. Evaluate whether you want to make the changes they suggest, then practice the changes on others within this circle.

Stretch the Boundaries of Your Networking Circle of Confidence

Once you have refined the promotional tools you will use to accomplish your networking goals, you will want to make additional contacts. Because you will not know most of these people, it will be a less comfortable activity to undertake. The practice that you gained with your inner circle of trusted friends should have prepared you to now move outside of that comfort zone.

It is said that any information a person needs is only two phone calls away, but the information cannot be gained until you (1) make a reasonable guess about who might have the information you need and (2) pick up the telephone to make the call. Using your network list that includes alumni, instructors, supervisors, employers, and associations, you can begin preparing your list of questions that will allow you to get the information you need. Review the following question list and then develop a list of your own.

Questions You Might Want to Ask

1. In the position you now hold, what do you do on a typical day?

2. What are the most interesting aspects of your job?

3. What part of your work do you consider dull or repetitious?

4. What were the jobs you had that led to your present position?

5. How long does it usually take to move from one step to the next in this career path?

6. What is the top position to which you can aspire in this career path?

7. What is the next step in *your* career path?

8. Are there positions in this field that are similar to your position?

9. What are the required qualifications and training for entry-level positions in this field?

10. Are there specific courses a student should take to be qualified to work in this field?

11. What are the entry-level jobs in this field?

12. What types of training are provided to persons entering this field?

13. What are the salary ranges your organization typically offers to entry-level candidates for positions in this field?

14. What special advice would you give a person entering this field?

15. Do you see this field as a growing one?

16. How do you see the content of the entry-level jobs in this field changing over the next two years?

17. What can I do to prepare myself for these changes?

18. What is the best way to obtain a position that will start me on a career in this field?

19. Do you have any information on job specifications and descriptions that I may have?

20. What related occupational fields would you suggest I explore?

21. How could I improve my resume for a career in this field?

22. Who else would you suggest I talk to, both in your organization and in other organizations?

Questions You Might Have to Answer

In order to communicate effectively, you must anticipate questions that will be asked of you by the networkers you contact. Review the list below and see if you can easily answer each of these questions. If you cannot, it may be time to revisit the self-assessment process.

1. Where did you get my name? or How did you find out about this organization?

2. What are your career goals?

3. What kind of job are you interested in?

4. What do you know about this organization and this industry?

5. How do you know you're prepared to undertake an entry-level position in this industry?

6. What course work have you taken that is related to your career interests?

7. What are your short-term career goals?

8. What are your long-term career goals?

9. Do you plan to obtain additional formal education?

10. What contributions have you made to previous employers?

11. Which of your previous jobs have you enjoyed the most, and why?

12. What are you particularly good at doing?

13. What shortcomings have you had to face in previous employment?

14. What are your three greatest strengths?

15. How comfortable do you feel with your communication style?

General Networking Tips

Make Every Contact Count. Setting the tone for each interaction is critical. Approaches that will help you communicate in an effective way include politeness, being appreciative of time provided to you, and being prepared and thorough. Remember, *everyone* within an organization has a circle of influence, so be prepared to interact effectively with each person you encounter in the networking process, including secretarial and support staff. Many information or job seekers have thwarted their own efforts by being rude to some individuals they encountered as they networked because they made the incorrect assumption that certain persons were unimportant.

Sometimes your contacts may be surprised at their ability to help you. After meeting and talking with you, they might think they have not offered much in the way of help. A day or two later, however, they may make a contact that would be useful to you and refer you to it.

With Each Contact, Widen Your Circle of Networkers. Always leave an informational interview with the names of at least two more people who can help you get the information or job that you are seeking. Don't be shy about asking for additional contacts; networking is all about increasing the number of people you can interact with to achieve your goals.

Make Your Own Decisions. As you talk with different people and get answers to the questions you pose, you may hear conflicting information or get conflicting suggestions. Your job is to listen to these "experts" and decide what information and which suggestions will help you achieve *your* goals. Only implement those suggestions that you believe will work for you.

SHUTTING DOWN YOUR NETWORK

As you achieve the goals that motivated your networking activity—getting the information you need or the job you want—the time will come to inactivate all or parts of your network. As you do so, be sure to tell your primary supporters about your change in status. Call or write to each one of them and give them as many details about your new status as you feel is necessary to maintain a positive relationship.

Because a network takes on a life of its own, activity undertaken on your behalf will continue even after you cease your efforts. As you get calls or are contacted in some fashion, be sure to inform these networkers about your change in status, and thank them for assistance they have provided.

Information on the latest employment trends indicates that workers will change jobs or careers several times in their lifetime. If you carefully and thoughtfully conduct your networking activities now, you will have solid experience when you need to network again.

CHAPTER FIVE

INTERVIEWING

Certainly, there can be no one part of the job search process more fraught with anxiety and worry than the interview. Yet seasoned job seekers welcome the interview and will often say, "Just get me an interview and I'm on my way!" They understand that the interview is crucial to the hiring process and equally crucial for them, as job candidates, to have the opportunity for a personal dialogue to add to what the employer may already have learned from a resume, cover letter, and telephone conversations.

Believe it or not, the interview is to be welcomed, and even enjoyed! It is a perfect opportunity for you, the candidate, to sit down with an employer and express yourself and display who you are and what you want. Of course, it takes thought and planning and a little strategy; after all, it *is* a job interview! But it can be a positive, if not pleasant, experience and one you can look back on and feel confident about.

For many new job seekers, a job, any job, seems a wonderful thing. But interview veterans know that the job interview is an important step for both sides—the employer and the candidate—to see what each has to offer and whether there is going to be a fit of personalities, work styles, and attitudes. And it is this concept of balance in the interview, that both sides have important parts to play, that holds the key to success in mastering this aspect of the job search strategy.

Try to think of the interview as a conversation between two interested and equal partners. You both have important, even vital, information to deliver and learn. Of course, there's no denying the employer has some leverage, especially in the initial interview for recruitment or any interview scheduled by the candidate and not the recruiter. That should not prevent the interviewee from seeking to play an equal part in what should be a fair exchange of information. Too often the untutored candidate allows the interview to become one-sided. The employer asks all the questions and the candidate simply responds. The ideal would be for two mutually interested parties to sit down and discuss possibilities for each. This is a *conversation of significance,* and it requires pre-interview preparation, thought about the tone of the interview, and planning of the nature and details of the information to be exchanged.

PREPARING FOR THE INTERVIEW

Most initial interviews are about thirty minutes long. Given the brevity, the information that is exchanged ought to be important. The candidate should be delivering material that the employer cannot discover on the resume, and, in turn, the candidate should be learning things about the employer that he or she could not otherwise find out. After all, if you have only thirty minutes, why waste time on information that is already published? The information exchanged is more than just factual, and both sides will learn much from what they see of each other, as well. How the candidate looks, speaks, and acts is important to the employer. The employer's attention to the interview and awareness of the candidate's resume, the setting, and the quality of information presented are important to the candidate.

Just as the employer has every right to be disappointed when a prospect is late for the interview, looks unkempt, and seems ill-prepared to answer fairly standard questions, the candidate may be disappointed with an interviewer who isn't ready for the meeting, hasn't learned the basic resume facts, and is constantly interrupted for telephone calls. In either situation, there's good reason to feel let down.

There are many elements to a successful interview, and some of them are not easy to describe or prepare for. Sometimes there is just a chemistry between interviewer and interviewee that brings out the best in both, and a good exchange takes place. But there is much the candidate can do to pave the way for success in terms of his or her resume, personal appearance, goals, and interview strategy—each of which we will discuss. However, none of this preparation is as important as the time and thought the candidate gives to personal self-assessment.

Self-Assessment

Neither a stunning resume nor an expensive, well-tailored suit can compensate for candidates who do not know what they want, where they are going, or why they are interviewing with a particular employer. Self-assessment, the process by which we begin to know and acknowledge our own particular blend of education, experiences, needs, and goals, is not something that can be sorted out the weekend before a major interview. Of all the elements of interview preparation, this one requires the longest lead time and cannot be faked.

Because the time allotted for most interviews is brief, it is all the more important for job candidates to understand and express succinctly why they are there and what they have to offer. This is not a time for undue modesty (or for braggadocio either); but it is a time for a compelling, reasoned statement of why you feel that you and this employer might make a good match. It means you have to have thought about your skills, interests, and attributes; related those to your life experiences and your own history of challenges and opportunities; and determined what that indicates about your strengths, preferences, values, and areas needing further development.

A common complaint of employers is that many candidates don't take advantage of the interview time and don't seem to know why they are there or what they want. When candidates are asked to talk about themselves and their work-related skills and attributes, employers don't want to be faced with shyness or embarrassed laughter; they need to know about you so they can make a fair determination of you and your competition. If you lose the opportunity to make a case for your employability, you can be certain the person ahead of you has or the person after you will. It will be on the strength of those impressions that the employer will hire.

If you need some assistance with self-assessment issues, refer to Chapter 1. Included are suggested exercises that can be done as needed, such as making up an experiential diary and extracting obvious strengths and weaknesses from past experiences. These simple, pen-and-paper assignments will help you look at past activities as collections of tasks with accompanying skills and responsibilities. Don't overlook your high school or college career office. Many offer personal counseling on self-assessment issues and may provide testing instruments such as the Myers-Briggs Type Indicator (MBTI), the Harrington-O'Shea Career Decision Making System (CDM), the Strong Interest Inventory (SII), or any of a wide selection of assessment tools that can help you clarify some of these issues prior to the interview stage of your job search.

The Resume

Resume preparation has been discussed in detail, and some basic examples of various types were provided. In this section, we want to concentrate on how best to use your resume in the interview. In most cases, the employer will have seen the resume prior to the interview, and, in fact, it may well have been the quality of that resume that secured the interview opportunity.

An interview is a conversation, however, and not an exercise in reading. So, if the employer hasn't seen your resume and you have brought it along to the interview, wait until asked or until the end of the interview to offer it. Otherwise, you may find yourself staring at the back of your resume and simply answering "yes" and "no" to a series of questions drawn from that document.

Sometimes an interviewer is not prepared and does not know or recall the contents of the resume and may use the resume to a greater or lesser degree as a prompt during the interview. It is for you to judge what that may indicate about the individual doing the interview or the employer. If your interviewer seems surprised by the scheduled meeting, relies on the resume to an inordinate degree, and seems otherwise unfamiliar with your background, this lack of preparation for the hiring process could well be a symptom of general management disorganization or may simply be the result of poor planning on the part of one individual. It is your responsibility as a potential employee to be aware of these signals and make your decisions accordingly.

··

In any event, it is perfectly acceptable for you to get the conversation back to a more interpersonal style by saying something like, "Mr. Jones, you might be interested in some recent design experience I gained in an internship that is not detailed on my resume. May I tell you about it?" This can return the interview to two people talking to each other, not one reading and the other responding.

··

By all means, bring at least one copy of your resume to the interview. Occasionally, at the close of an interview, an interviewer will express an interest in circulating a resume to several departments, and you could then offer to provide copies. Sometimes an interview appointment provides an opportunity to meet others in the organization who may express an interest in you and your background, and it may be helpful to follow that up with a copy of your resume. Our best advice, however, is to keep it out of sight until needed or requested.

Appearance

Although many of the absolute rules that once dominated the advice offered to job candidates about appearance have now been moderated significantly, conservative is still the watchword unless you are interviewing in a fashion-related industry. For men, conservative translates into a well-cut dark suit with appropriate tie, hosiery, and dress shirt. A wise strategy for the male job seeker looking for a good but not expensive suit would be to try the men's department of a major department store. They usually carry a good range of sizes, fabrics, and prices; offer professional sales help; provide free tailoring; and have associated departments for putting together a professional look.

For women, there is more latitude. Business suits are still popular, but they have become more feminine in color and styling with a variety of jacket and skirt lengths. In addition to suits, better-quality dresses are now worn in many environments and, with the correct accessories, can be most appropriate. Company literature, professional magazines, the business section of major newspapers, and television interviews can all give clues about what is being worn in different employer environments.

Both men and women need to pay attention to issues such as hair, jewelry, and makeup; these are often what separates the candidate in appearance from the professional workforce. It seems particularly difficult for the young job seeker to give up certain hair styles, eyeglass fashions, and jewelry habits, yet those can be important to the employer, who is concerned with your ability to successfully make the transition into the organization. Candidates often find the best strategy is to dress conservatively until they find employment. Once employed and familiar with the norms within your organization, you can begin to determine a look that you enjoy, works for you, and fits your organization.

Choose clothes that suit your body type, fit well, and flatter you. Feel good about the way you look! The interview day is not the best for a new hairdo, a new pair of shoes, or any other change that will distract you or cause you to be self-conscious. Arrive a bit early to avoid being rushed, and ask the receptionist to direct you to a restroom for any last-minute adjustments of hair and clothes.

Employer Information

Whether your interview is for graduate school admission, an overseas corporate position, or a lab position with a local company, it is important to know something about the employer or the organization. Keeping in mind that the interview is relatively brief and that you will hopefully have other interviews with other organizations, it is important to keep your research in proportion. If secondary interviews are called for, you will have additional time to do further research. For the first interview, it is helpful to know the organization's mission, goals, size, scope of operations, etc. Your research may uncover recent areas of challenge or particular successes that may help to fuel the interview. Use the "Where Are These Jobs, Anyway?" section of Chapter 3, your library, and your career or guidance office to help you locate this information in the most efficient way possible. Don't be shy in asking advice of these counseling and guidance professionals on how best to spend your preparation time. With some practice, you'll soon learn how much information is enough and which kinds of information are most useful to you.

INTERVIEW CONTENT

We've already discussed how it can help to think of the interview as an important conversation—one that, as with any conversation, you want to find pleasant and interesting and to leave you with a good feeling. But because this conversation is especially important, the information that's exchanged is critical to its success. What do you want them to know about you? What do you need to know about them? What interview technique do you need to particularly pay attention to? How do you want to manage the close of the interview? What steps will follow in the hiring process?

Except for the professional interviewer, most of us find interviewing stressful and anxiety-provoking. Developing a strategy before you begin interviewing will help you relieve some stress and anxiety. One particular strategy that has worked for many and may work for you is interviewing by objective. Before you interview, write down three to five goals you would like to achieve for that interview. They may be technique goals: smile a little more, have a firmer handshake, be sure to ask about the next stage in the interview process before leaving, etc. They may be content-oriented goals: find out about the company's current challenges and opportunities, be sure to speak of my recent research writing experiences or foreign travel, etc. Whatever your goals, jot down a few of them as goals for this interview.

Most people find that, in trying to achieve these few goals, their interviewing technique becomes more organized and focused. After the interview, the most common question friends and family ask is "How did it go?" With this technique, you have an indication of whether you met *your* goals for the meeting, not just some vague idea of how it went. Chances are, if you accomplished what you wanted to, it informed the quality of the entire interview. As you continue to interview, you will want to revise your goals to continue improving your interview skills.

Now, add to the concept of the significant conversation the idea of a beginning, a middle, and a closing and you will have two thoughts that will give your interview a distinctive character. Be sure to make your introduction warm and cordial. Say your full name (and if it's a difficult-to-pronounce name, help the interviewer to pronounce it) and make certain you know your interviewer's name and how to pronounce it. Most interviews begin with some "soft talk" about the weather, chat about the candidate's trip to the interview site, national events, etc. This is done as a courtesy to relax both you and the interviewer, to get you talking, and to generally try to defuse the atmosphere of excessive tension. Try to be yourself, engage in the conversation, and don't try to second-guess the interviewer. This is simply what it appears to be—casual conversation.

Once you and the interviewer move on to exchange more serious information in the middle part of the interview, the two most important concerns become your ability to handle challenging questions and your success at asking meaningful ones. Interviewer questions will probably fall into one of three categories: personal assessment and career direction, academic background, and knowledge of the employer. The following are some examples of questions in each category:

Personal Assessment and Career Direction

1. How would you describe yourself?

2. What motivates you to put forth your greatest effort?

3. In what kind of work environment are you most comfortable?

4. What do you consider to be your greatest strengths and weaknesses?

5. How well do you work under pressure?

6. What qualifications do you have that make you think you will be successful in this career?

7. Will you relocate? What do you feel would be the most difficult aspect of relocating?

8. Are you willing to travel?

9. Why should I hire you?

Academic Background

1. Why did you select your college or university?

2. What changes would you make at your alma mater?

3. What led you to choose your major?

4. What subjects did you like best and least? Why?

5. If you could, how would you plan your academic study differently? Why?

6. Describe your most rewarding college experience.

7. How has your college experience prepared you for this career?

8. Do you think that your grades are a good indication of your ability to succeed with this organization?

9. Do you have plans for continued study?

Knowledge of the Employer

1. If you were hiring a graduate of your school for this position, what qualities would you look for?

2. What do you think it takes to be successful in an organization like ours?

3. In what ways do you think you can make a contribution to our organization?

4. Why did you choose to seek a position with this organization?

The interviewer wants a response to each question but is also gauging your enthusiasm, preparedness, and willingness to communicate. In each response you should provide some information about yourself that can be related to the employer's needs. A common mistake is to give too much information. Answer each question completely, but be careful not to run on too long with extensive details or examples.

Questions About Underdeveloped Skills

Most employers interview people who have met some minimum criteria of education and experience. They interview candidates to see who they are, to learn what kind of personality they exhibit, and to get some sense of how this person might fit into the existing organization. It may be that you are asked about skills the employer hopes to find and that you have not documented. Maybe it's grant-writing experience, knowledge of the European political system, or a knowledge of the film world.

To questions about skills and experiences you don't have, answer honestly and forthrightly and try to offer some additional information about skills you do have. For example, perhaps the employer is disappointed you have no grant-writing experience. An honest answer may be as follows:

> No, unfortunately, I was never in a position to acquire those skills. I do understand something of the complexities of the grant-writing process and feel confident that my attention to detail, careful reading skills, and strong writing would make grants a wonderful challenge in a new job. I think I could get up on the learning curve quickly.

The employer hears an honest admission of lack of experience but is reassured by some specific skill details that do relate to grant writing and a confident manner that suggests enthusiasm and interest in a challenge.

For many students, questions about their possible contribution to an employer's organization can prove challenging. Because your education has probably not included specific training for a job, you need to review your academic record and select capabilities you have developed in your major that an employer can appreciate. For example, perhaps you read well and can analyze and condense what you've read into smaller, more focused pieces. That could be valuable. Or maybe you did some serious research and you know you have valuable investigative skills. Your public speaking might be highly developed and you might use visual aids appropriately and effectively. Or maybe your skill at correspondence, memos, and messages is effective. Whatever it is, you must take it out of the academic context and put it into a new, employer-friendly context so your interviewer can best judge how you could help the organization.

Exhibiting knowledge of the organization will, without a doubt, show the interviewer that you are interested enough in the available position to have done some legwork in preparation for the interview. Remember, it is not necessary to know every detail of the organization's history, but rather to have a general knowledge about why it is in business and how the industry is faring.

Sometime during the interview, generally after the midway point, you'll be asked if you have any questions for the interviewer. Your questions will tell the employer much about your attitude and your desire to understand the organization's expectations so you can compare it to your own strengths. The following are some selected questions you might want to ask:

1. What are the main responsibilities of the position?

2. What are the opportunities and challenges associated with this position?

3. Could you outline some possible career paths beginning with this position?

4. How regularly do performance evaluations occur?

5. What is the communication style of the organization? (Meetings, memos, etc.)

6. What would a typical day in this position be like for me?

7. What kinds of opportunities might exist for me to improve my professional skills within the organization?

8. What have been some of the interesting challenges and opportunities your organization has recently faced?

Most interviews draw to a natural closing point, so be careful not to prolong the discussion. At a signal from the interviewer, wind up your presentation, express your appreciation for the opportunity, and be sure to ask what the next stage in the process will be. When can you expect to hear from them?

Will they be conducting second-tier interviews? If you're interested and haven't heard, would they mind a phone call? Be sure to collect a business card with the name and phone number of your interviewer. On your way out, you might have an opportunity to pick up organizational literature you haven't seen before.

With the right preparation—a thorough self-assessment, professional clothing, and employer information—you'll be able to set and achieve the goals you have established for the interview process.

CHAPTER SIX

NETWORKING OR INTERVIEWING FOLLOW-UP

Quite often there is a considerable time lag between interviewing for a position and being hired, or, in the case of the networker, between your phone call or letter to a possible contact and the opportunity of a meeting. This can be frustrating. "Why aren't they contacting me?" "I thought I'd get another interview, but no one has telephoned." "Am I out of the running?" You don't know what is happening.

CONSIDER THE DIFFERING PERSPECTIVES

Of course, there is another perspective—that of the network contact or hiring organization. Organizations are complex with multiple tasks that need to be accomplished each day. Hiring is but one discrete activity that does not occur as frequently as other job assignments. The hiring process might have to take second place to other, more immediate organizational needs. Although it may be very important to you and it is certainly ultimately significant to the employer, other issues such as fiscal management, planning and product development, employer vacation periods, or financial constraints may prevent an organization or individual within that organization from acting on your employment or your request for information as quickly as you or they would prefer.

USE YOUR COMMUNICATION SKILLS

Good communication is essential here to resolve any anxieties, and the responsibility is on you, the job or information seeker. Too many job seekers and networkers offer as an excuse that they don't want to "bother" the organization by writing letters or calling. Let us assure you here and now, once and for all, that if you are troubling an organization by overcommunicating, someone will indicate that situation to you quite clearly. If not, you can only assume you are a worthwhile prospect and the employer appreciates being reminded of your availability and interest in them. Let's look at follow-up practices in both the job interview process and the networking situation separately.

FOLLOWING UP ON THE EMPLOYMENT INTERVIEW

A brief thank-you note following an interview is an excellent and polite way to begin a series of follow-up communications with a potential employer with whom you have interviewed and want to remain in touch. It should be just that—a thank you for good meeting. If you failed to mention some fact or experience during your interview that you think might add to your candidacy, you may use this note to do that. However, this should be essentially a note whose overall tone is appreciative and, if appropriate, indicative of a continuing interest in pursuing any opportunity that may exist with that organization. It is one of the few pieces of business correspondence that may be handwritten, but always use plain, good quality, monarch-size paper.

If, however, at this point you are no longer interested in the employer, the thank-you note is an appropriate time to indicate that. You are under no obligation to identify any reason for not continuing to pursue employment with that organization, but if you are so inclined to indicate your professional reasons (pursuing other employers more akin to your interests, looking for greater income production than this employer can provide, a different geographic location than is available, etc.), you certainly may. It should not be written with an eye to negotiation, for it will not be interpreted as such.

As part of your interview closing, you should have taken the initiative to establish lines of communication for continuing information about your candidacy. If you asked permission to telephone, wait a week following your thank-you note, then telephone your contact simply to inquire how things are progressing on your employment status. The feedback you receive here should be taken at face value. If your interviewer simply has no information, he or she will tell you so and indicate whether you should call again and when. Don't be discouraged if this should continue over some period of time.

If during this time something occurs that you think improves or changes your candidacy (some new qualification or experience you may have had), including any offers from other organizations, by all means telephone or write to inform the employer about this. In the case of an offer from a competing but less desirable or equally desirable organization, telephone your contact, explain what has happened, express your real interest in the organization, and inquire whether some determination on your employment might be made before you must respond to this other offer. If the organization is truly interested in you, they may be moved to make a decision about your candidacy. Equally possible is the scenario in which they are not yet ready to make a decision and so advise you to take the offer that has been presented. Again, you have no ethical alternative but to deal with the information presented in a straightforward manner.

When accepting other employment, be sure to contact any employers still actively considering you and inform them of your new job. Thank them graciously for their consideration. There are many other job seekers out there just like you who will benefit from having their candidacy improved when others bow out of the race. Who knows, you might at some future time have occasion to interact professionally with one of the organizations with whom you sought employment. How embarrassing to have someone remember you as the candidate who failed to notify them of taking a job elsewhere!

In all of your follow-up communications, keep good notes of who you spoke with, when you called, and any instructions that were given about return communications. This will prevent any misunderstandings and provide you with good records of what has transpired.

FOLLOWING UP ON THE NETWORK CONTACT

Far more common than the forgotten follow-up after an interview is the situation where a good network contact is allowed to lapse. Good communications are the essence of a network, and follow-up is not so much a matter of courtesy here as it is a necessity. In networking for job information and contacts, you are the active network link. Without you, and without continual contact from you, there is no network. You and your need for employment is often the only shared element between members of the network. Because network contacts were made regardless of the availability of any particular employment, it is incumbent upon the job seeker, if not simple common sense, that unless you stay in regular communication with the network, you will not be available for consideration should some job become available in the future.

This brings up the issue of responsibility, which is likewise very clear. The job seeker initiates network contacts and is responsible for maintaining those contacts; therefore, the entire responsibility for the network belongs with him or her. This becomes patently obvious if the network is left unattended. It very shortly falls out of existence because it cannot survive without careful attention by the networker.

A variety of ways are open to you to keep the lines of communication open and to attempt to interest the network in you as a possible employee. You are limited only by your own enthusiasm for members of the network and your creativity. However, you as a networker are well advised to keep good records of whom you have met and spoken with in each organization. Be sure to send thank-you notes to anyone who has spent any time with you, be it a quick tour of a department or a sit-down informational interview. All of these communications should, in addition to their ostensible reason, add some information about you and your particular combination of strengths and attributes.

You can contact your network at any time to convey continued interest, to comment on some recent article you came across concerning an organization, to add information about your training or changes in your qualifications, to ask advice or seek guidance in your job search, or to request referrals to other possible network opportunities. Sometimes just a simple note to network members reminding them of your job search, indicating that you have been using their advice, and noting that you are still actively pursuing leads and hope to continue to interact with them is enough to keep communications alive.

Because networks have been abused in the past, it's important that your conduct be above reproach. Networks are exploratory options, they are not backdoor access to employers. The network works best for someone who is exploring a new industry or making a transition into a new area of employment and who needs to find information or to alert people to his or her search activity. Always be candid and direct with contacts in expressing the purpose of your call or letter and your interest in their help or information about their organization. In follow-up contacts keep the tone professional and direct. Your honesty will be appreciated, and people will respond as best they can if your qualifications appear to meet their forthcoming needs. The network does not owe you anything, and that tone should be clear to each person you meet.

FEEDBACK FROM FOLLOW-UPS

A network contact may prove to be miscalculated. Perhaps you were referred to someone and it became clear that your goals and his or her particular needs did not make a good match. Or the network contact may simply not be in a position to provide you with the information you are seeking. Or in some unfortunate situations, the contact may become annoyed by being contacted for this purpose. In such a situation, many job seekers simply say "Thank you" and move on.

If the contact is simply not the right contact, but the individual you are speaking with is not annoyed by the call, it might be a better tactic to express regret that the contact was misplaced and then express to the contact what you are seeking and ask for his or her advice or possible suggestions as to a next step. The more people who are aware you are seeking employment, the better your chances of connecting, and that is the purpose of a network. Most people in a profession have excellent knowledge of their field and varying amounts of expertise on areas near to or tangent to their own. Use their expertise and seek some guidance before you dissolve the contact. You may be pleasantly surprised.

Occasionally, networkers will express the feeling that they have done as much as they can or provided all the information that is available to them. This may be a cue that they would like to be released from your network. Be alert to such attempts to terminate, graciously thank the individual by letter, and move on in your network development. A network is always changing, adding and losing members, and you want the network to be composed only of those who are actively interested in supporting your interests.

A FINAL POINT ON NETWORKING FOR ECONOMICS MAJORS

In any of the fields an economics major might consider as a potential career path, it's important to remember that networkers and interviewers will be critically evaluating all of your written and oral communications. This should serve to emphasize the importance of the quality of your interactions with people in a position to help you in your job search. Communications skills are vital to success in economics careers.

In your telephone communications, interview presentation, follow-up correspondence, and ability to deal with negative feedback, your warmth, style, and personality as evidenced in your spoken and written use of English will be part of the portfolio of impressions you create with the people you meet along the way.

CHAPTER SEVEN

JOB OFFER CONSIDERATIONS

for many recent college graduates, the thrill of their first job and, for some, the most substantial regular income they have ever earned seems an excess of good fortune coming at once. To question that first income or be critical in any way of the conditions of employment at the time of the initial offer seems like looking a gift horse in the mouth. It doesn't seem to occur to many new hires even to attempt to negotiate any aspect of their first job. And, as many employers who deal with entry-level jobs for recent college graduates will readily confirm, the reality is that there simply isn't much movement in salary available to these new college recruits. The entry-level hire generally does not have an employment track record on a professional level to provide any leverage for negotiation. Real negotiations on salary, benefits, retirement provisions, etc., come to those with significant employment records at higher income levels.

Of course, the job offer is more than just money. It can be comprised of geographic assignment, duties and responsibilities, training, benefits, health and medical insurance, educational assistance, car allowance or company vehicle, and a host of other items. All of this is generally detailed in the formal letter that presents the final job offer. In most cases, this is a follow-up to a personal phone call from the employer representative who has been principally responsible for your hiring process.

That initial telephone offer is certainly binding as a verbal agreement, but most firms follow up with a detailed letter outlining the most significant parts of your employment contract. You may certainly choose to respond immediately at the time of the telephone offer (which would be considered a binding oral contract), but you will also be required to formally answer the letter of offer with a letter of acceptance, restating the salient elements of the employer's description of your position, salary, and benefits. This ensures that both parties are clear on the terms and conditions of employment and remuneration and any other outstanding aspects of the job offer.

IS THIS THE JOB YOU WANT?

Most new employees will write this letter of acceptance back, glad to be in the position to accept employment. If you've worked hard to get the offer and the job market is tight, other offers may not be in sight, so you will say, "Yes, I accept!" What is important here is that the job offer you accept be one that does fit your particular needs, values, and interests as you've outlined them in your self-assessment process. Moreover, it should be a job that will not only use your skills and education, but also challenge you to develop new skills and talents.

Jobs are sometimes accepted too hastily, for the wrong reasons, and without proper scrutiny by the applicant. For example, an individual might readily accept a sales job only to find the continual rejection by potential clients unendurable. An office worker might realize within weeks the constraints of a desk job and yearn for more activity. Employment is an important part of our lives. It is, for most of our adult lives, our most continuous productive activity. We want to make good choices based on the right criteria.

If you have a low tolerance for risk, a job based on commission will certainly be very anxiety provoking. If being near your family is important, issues of relocation could present a decision crisis for you. If you're an adventurous person, a job with frequent travel would provide needed excitement and be very desirable. The importance of income, the need to continue your education, your personal health situation—all of these have an impact on whether the job you are considering will ultimately meet your needs. Unless you've spent some time understanding and thinking about these issues, it will be difficult to evaluate offers you do receive.

More importantly, if you make a decision that you cannot tolerate and feel you must leave that job, you will then have both unemployment and self-esteem issues to contend with. These will combine to make the next job search tough going, indeed. So make your acceptance a carefully considered decision.

NEGOTIATING YOUR OFFER

It may be that there is some aspect of your job offer that is not particularly attractive to you. Perhaps there is no relocation allotment to help you move your possessions, and this presents some financial hardship for you. It may be that the medical and health insurance is less than you had hoped. Your initial assignment may be different than you expected, either in its location or in the duties and responsibilities that comprise it. Or it may simply be that the salary is less than you anticipated. Other considerations may be your official starting date of employment, vacation time, evening hours, dates of training programs or schools, etc.

If you are considering not accepting the job because of some item or items in the job offer "package" that do not meet your needs, you should know that most employers emphatically wish that you would bring that issue to their attention. It may be that the employer can alter it to make the offer more agreeable for you. In some cases it cannot be changed. In any event the employer would generally like to have the opportunity to try to remedy a difficulty rather than risk losing a good potential employee over an issue that might have been resolved. After all, they have spent time and funds in securing your services, and they certainly deserve an opportunity to resolve any possible differences.

Honesty is the best approach in discussing any objections or uneasiness you might have over the employer's offer. Having received your formal offer in writing, contact your employer representative and indicate your particular dissatisfaction in a straightforward manner. For example, you might explain that, while very interested in being employed by this organization, the salary (or any other benefit) is less than you have determined you require. State the terms you do need, and listen to the response. You may be asked to put this in writing, or you may be asked to hold off until the firm can decide on a response. If you are dealing with a senior representative of the organization, one who has been involved in hiring for some time, you may get an immediate response or a solid indication of possible outcomes.

Perhaps the issue is one of relocation. Your initial assignment is in the Midwest, and because you had indicated a strong West Coast preference, you are surprised at the actual assignment. You might simply indicate that, while you understand the need for the company to assign you based on its needs, you are disappointed and had hoped to be placed on the West Coast. You could inquire if that were still possible and, if not, would it be reasonable to expect a West Coast relocation in the future.

If your request is presented in a reasonable way, most employers will not see this as jeopardizing your offer. If they can agree to your proposal, they will. If not, they will simply tell you so, and you may choose to continue your candidacy with them or remove yourself from consideration as a possible employee. The choice will be up to you.

Some firms will adjust benefits within their parameters to meet the candidate's need if at all possible. If a candidate requires a relocation cost allowance, he or she may be asked to forgo tuition benefits for the first year to accomplish this adjustment. An increase in life insurance may be adjusted by some other benefit trade-off; perhaps a family dental plan is not needed. In these decisions, you are called upon, sometimes under time pressure, to know how you value these issues and how important each is to you.

Many employers find they are more comfortable negotiating for candidates who have unique qualifications or who bring especially needed expertise to the organization. Employers hiring large numbers of entry-level college graduates may be far more reluctant to accommodate any changes in offer conditions. They are well supplied with candidates with similar education and experience, so that if rejected by one candidate, they can draw new candidates from an ample labor pool.

COMPARING OFFERS

With only about 40 percent of recent college graduates employed three months after graduation, many graduates do not get to enjoy the experience of entertaining more than one offer at a time. The conditions of the economy, the job seeker's particular geographic job market, and her or his own needs and demands for certain employment conditions may not provide more than one offer at a time. Some job seekers may feel that no reasonable offer should go unaccepted for the simple fear there won't be another.

In a tough job market, or if the job you seek is not widely available, or when your job search goes on too long and becomes difficult to sustain financially and emotionally, it may be necessary to accept an offer. The alternative is continued unemployment. Even here, when you feel you don't have a choice, you can at least understand that in accepting this particular offer, there may be limitations and conditions you don't appreciate. At the time of acceptance, there were no other alternatives, but the new employee can begin to use that position to gain the experience and talent to move toward a more attractive position.

Sometimes, however, more than one offer is received at one time, and the candidate has the luxury of choice. If the job seeker knows what he or she wants and has done the necessary self-assessment honestly and thoroughly, it may be clear that one of the offers conforms more closely to those expressed wants and needs.

However, if, as so often happens, the offers are similar in terms of conditions and salary, the question then becomes which organization might provide the necessary climate, opportunities, and advantages for your professional development and growth. This is the time when solid employer research and astute questioning during the interviews really pays off. How much did you learn about the employer through your own research and skillful questioning?

When the interviewer asked during the interview "Do you have any questions?" did you ask the kinds of questions that would help resolve a choice between one organization and another? Just as an employer must decide among numerous applicants, so must the applicant learn to assess the potential employer. Both are partners in the job search.

RENEGING ON AN OFFER

An especially disturbing occurrence for employers and career counseling professionals is when a job seeker formally (either orally or by written contract) accepts employment with one organization and later reneges on the agreement and goes with another employer.

There are all kinds of rationalizations offered for this unethical behavior. None of them satisfies. The sad irony is that what the job seeker is willing to do to a potential employer—make a promise and then break it—would outrage the job seeker—e.g., if a potential employer pulled the job offer. It is a very bad way to begin a career. It suggests the individual has not taken the time to do the necessary self-assessment and self-awareness exercises to think and judge critically. The new offer taken may, in fact, be no better or worse than the one refused. Job candidates should be aware that there have been incidents of legal action following job candidates reneging on an offer. This adds a very sour note to what should be a harmonious beginning of a lifelong adventure.

CHAPTER EIGHT

THE GRADUATE SCHOOL CHOICE

The reasons for continuing one's education in graduate school can be as varied and unique as the individuals electing this course of action. Many continue their studies at an advanced level because they simply find it difficult to end the educational process. They love what they are learning and want to learn more and continue their academic exploration.

Studying a particular subject in great depth, discovering and testing the relationships that exist in markets, and writing critically on what others have discovered can present excitement, challenge, and serious work. Some economics majors have loved this aspect of their academic work and want to continue it. Others go on to graduate school for purely practical reasons; they have examined employment prospects in their field of study, and all indications are that a graduate degree is requisite for the type of job they seek. If you have earned a B.A. or B.S. in economics as a stepping stone to a career in government or law, for example, going on for further training is mandatory. As a bachelor's-level economics major, you realize you cannot move much above the assistant level without a master's degree or even a doctorate.

Alumni who are working in universities, government, health care, insurance, banking and finance, or investment firms can be a good source of information about what degree level the fields require for hiring. Ask your college career office for some alumni names to call or E-mail. Prepare some questions on specific job prospects in their field at each degree level. Examining the marketplace and talking to employers and professors will give you a sense of the scope of employment for a bachelor's degree, master's degree, or doctorate.

College teaching usually requires an advanced degree. The more senior positions in the career paths outlined in this book require advanced education and perhaps some specialization in a subject area such as market research or labor relations.

CONSIDER YOUR MOTIVES

The answer to the question of "Why graduate school?" is a personal one for each applicant. Nevertheless, it is important to consider your motives carefully. Graduate school involves additional time out of the employment market, a high degree of critical evaluation, significant autonomy as you pursue your studies, and considerable financial expenditure. For some students in doctoral programs, there may be additional life choice issues, such as relationships, marriage, and parenthood, that may present real challenges while in a program of study. You would be well-advised to consider the following questions as you think about your decision to continue your studies.

Are You Postponing Some Tough Decisions by Going to School?

Graduate school is not a place to go to avoid life's problems. There is intense competition for graduate school slots and for the fellowships, scholarships, and financial aid available. This competition means extensive interviewing, resume submission, and essay writing that rivals corporate recruitment. Likewise, the graduate school process is a mentored one in which faculty stay aware of and involved in the academic progress of their students and continually challenge the quality of their work. Many graduate students are called upon to participate in teaching and professional writing and research as well.

In other words, this is no place to hide from the spotlight. Graduate students work very hard, and much is demanded of them individually. If you elect to go to graduate school to avoid the stresses and strains of the "real world," you will find no safe place in higher academics. Vivid accounts, both fiction and nonfiction, have depicted quite accurately the personal and professional demands of graduate school work.

The selection of graduate studies as a career option should be a positive choice—something you *want* to do. It shouldn't be selected as an escape from other, less attractive or more challenging options, nor should it be selected as the option of last resort (i.e., "I can't do anything else; I'd better just stay in school."). If you're in some doubt about the strength of your reasoning about continuing in school, discuss the issues with a career counselor. Together you can clarify your reasoning, and you'll get some sound feedback on what you're about to undertake.

On the other hand, staying on in graduate school because of a particularly poor employment market and a lack of jobs at entry-level positions has proven to be an effective "stalling" strategy. If you can afford it, pursuing a graduate degree immediately after your undergraduate education gives you a year or two to "wait out" a difficult economic climate while at the same time acquiring a potentially valuable credential.

Have You Done Some "Hands-On" Reality Testing?

There are experiential options available to give some reality to your decision-making process about graduate school. Internships or work in the field can give you a good idea about employment demands, conditions, and atmosphere.

Perhaps, as an economics major, you're considering a doctoral program with an eye to university teaching. Begin with your own college professors and ask them to talk to you about their own educational and career paths to their current teaching posts. They can also talk to you about the time they spend outside the classroom, in research activities, or in departmental meetings dealing with faculty and budget concerns.

Even by hearing the experience of only one professor, you have a stronger concept of the pace of the job, interaction with colleagues, subject matter, and pressure to do research and publish results. Talking to people and asking questions can give you a better understanding of the objective of your graduate study. For economics majors especially, the opportunity to do this kind of reality testing is invaluable. It demonstrates far more authoritatively than any other method what your real-world skills are, how they can be put to use, and what aspect of your academic preparation you rely on. It has been well documented that economics majors do well in occupations once they identify them. Internship experiences speed up that process and prevent the frustrating and expensive work of investigation that many graduates begin only after graduation.

....

Do You Need an Advanced Degree to Work in Your Field?

Certainly there are fields such as law, psychiatry, medicine, and college teaching that demand advanced degrees. Is the field of employment you're considering one that also puts a premium on an advanced degree? You may be surprised. Read the want ads in a number of major Sunday newspapers for positions you would enjoy. How many of those require an advanced degree?

Retailing, for example, has always put a premium on what people can do, rather than how much education they have had. Successful people in retailing come from all academic preparations. A Ph.D. in English may bring only prestige to the individual employed as a magazine researcher. It may not bring a more senior position or better pay. In fact, it may disqualify you for some jobs because an employer might believe you will be unhappy to be overqualified for a particular position. Or your motives in applying for the work may be misconstrued, and the employer might think you will only be working at this level until something better comes along. None of this may be true for you, but it comes about because you are working outside of the usual territory for that degree level.

When economic times are especially difficult, we tend to see stories featured about individuals with advanced degrees doing what is considered unsuitable work, such as the Ph.D. in English driving a cab or the Ph.D. in chemistry waiting tables. Actually, this is not particularly surprising when you consider that as your degree level advances, the job market narrows appreciably. At any one time, regardless of economic circumstances, there are only so many jobs for your particular level of expertise. If you cannot find employment for your advanced degree level, chances are you will be considered suspect for many other kinds of employment and may be forced into temporary work far removed from your original intention.

Before making an important decision such as graduate study, learn your options and carefully consider what you want to do with your advanced degree. Ask yourself whether it is reasonable to think you can achieve your goals. Will there be jobs when you graduate? Where will they be? What will they pay? How competitive will the market be at that time, based on current predictions?

If you're uncertain about the degree requirements for the fields you're interested in, you should check a publication such as the U.S. Department of Labor's *Occupational Outlook Handbook*. Each entry has a section on training and other qualifications that will indicate clearly what the minimum educational requirement is for employment, what degree is the standard, and what employment may be possible without the required credential.

For example, for physicists and astronomers, a doctoral degree in physics or a closely related field is essential. Certainly this is the degree of choice in academic institutions. However, the *Occupational Outlook Handbook* also indicates what kinds of employment may be available to individuals holding a master's or even a bachelor's degree in physics.

Have You Compared Your Expectations of What Graduate School Will Do for You with What It Has Done for Alumni of the Program You're Considering?

Most colleges and universities perform some kind of postgraduate survey of their students to ascertain where they are employed, what additional education they have received, and what levels of salary they are enjoying. Ask to see this information either from the university you are considering applying to or from your own alma mater, especially if it has a similar graduate program. Such surveys often reveal surprises about occupational decisions, salaries, and work satisfaction. This information may affect your decision.

The value of self-assessment (the process of examining and making decisions about your own hierarchy of values and goals) is especially important in this process of analyzing the desirability of possible career paths involving graduate education. Sometimes a job requiring advanced education seems to hold real promise but is disappointing in salary potential or number of opportunities available. Certainly it is better to research this information before embarking on a program of graduate studies. It may not change your mind about your decision, but by becoming better informed about your choice, you become better prepared for your future.

Have You Talked with People in Your Field to Explore What You Might Be Doing After Graduate School?

In pursuing your undergraduate degree, you will have come into contact with many individuals trained in the field you are considering. You might also have the opportunity to attend professional conferences, workshops, seminars, and job fairs where you can expand your network of contacts. Talk to them all! Find out about their individual career paths, discuss your own plans and hopes, get their feedback on the reality of your expectations, and heed their advice about your prospects. Each will have a unique tale to tell, and each will bring a different perspective on the current marketplace for the credentials you are seeking. Talking to enough people will make you an expert on what's out there.

Are You Excited by the Idea of Studying the Particular Field You Have in Mind?

This question may be the most important one of all. If you are going to spend several years in advanced study, perhaps engendering some debt or postponing some lifestyle decisions for an advanced degree, you simply ought to enjoy what you're doing. Examine your work in the discipline so far. Has it been fun? Have you found yourself exploring various paths of thought? Do you read in your area for fun? Do you enjoy talking about it, thinking about it, and sharing it with others? Advanced degrees often are the beginning of a lifetime's involvement with a particular subject. Choose carefully a field that will hold your interest and your enthusiasm.

It is fairly obvious by now that we think you should give some careful thought to your decision and take some action. If nothing else, do the following:

❑ Talk and question (remember to listen!)

❑ Reality-test

❑ Soul-search by yourself and/or with a person you trust

FINDING THE RIGHT PROGRAM FOR YOU: SOME CONSIDERATIONS

There are several important factors in coming to a sound decision about the right graduate program for you. You'll want to begin by locating institutions that offer appropriate programs, examining each of these programs and their requirements, undertaking the application process by obtaining catalogs and application materials, visiting campuses if possible, arranging for letters of recommendation, writing your application statement, and finally following up on your applications.

Locate Institutions with Appropriate Programs

Once you decide on a particular advanced degree, it's important to develop a list of schools offering such a degree program. Perhaps the best sources of graduate program information are Peterson's *Guides to Graduate Study*. Use these guides to build your list. In addition, you may want to consult the College Board's *Index of Majors and Graduate Degrees,* which will help you find graduate programs offering the degree you seek. It is indexed by academic major and then categorized by state.

Now, this may be a considerable list. You may want to narrow the choices down further by a number of criteria: tuition, availability of financial aid, public versus private institutions, U.S. versus international institutions, size of student body, size of faculty, application fee (this varies by school; most fall within the $20 to $75 range), and geographic location. This is only a partial list; you will have your own important considerations. Perhaps you are an avid scuba diver and you find it unrealistic to think you could pursue graduate study for a number of years without being able to ocean dive from time to time. Good! That's a decision and it's honest. Now, how far from the ocean is too far, and what schools meet your other needs? In any case, and according to your own criteria, begin to build a reasonable list of graduate schools that you are willing to spend the time investigating.

Examine the Degree Programs and Their Requirements

Once you've determined the criteria by which you want to develop a list of graduate schools, you can begin to examine the degree program requirements, faculty composition, and institutional research orientation. Again, using resources such as Peterson's *Guides to Graduate Study* can reveal an amazingly rich level of material by which to judge your possible selections.

In addition to degree programs and degree requirements, entries will include information about application fees, entrance test requirements, tuition, percentage of applicants accepted, numbers of applicants receiving financial aid, gender breakdown of students, numbers of full- and part-time faculty, and often gender breakdown of faculty as well. Numbers graduating in each program and research orientations of departments are also included in some entries. There is information on graduate housing, student services, and library, research, and computer facilities. A contact person, phone number, and address are also standard pieces of information in these listings. In addition to the standard entries, some schools pay an additional fee to place full-page, more detailed program descriptions. The location of such a display ad, if present, would be indicated at the end of the standard entry.

It can be helpful to draw up a chart and enter relevant information about each school you are considering in order to have a ready reference on points of information that are important to you.

Undertake the Application Process

The Catalog. Once you've decided on a selection of schools, send for catalogs and applications. It is important to note here that these materials might take many weeks to arrive. Consequently, if you need the materials quickly, it might be best to telephone and explain your situation to see whether the process can be speeded up for you. Also, check a local college or university library, which might have current and complete college catalogs in a microfiche collection. These microfiche copies can provide you with helpful information while you wait for your own copy of the graduate school catalog or bulletin to arrive.

When you receive your catalogs, give them a careful reading and make notes of issues you might want to discuss on the telephone or in a personal interview, if that's possible. Does the course selection have the depth you had hoped for?

What is the ratio of faculty to the required number of courses for your degree? How often will you encounter the same faculty member as an instructor? If, for example, your program offers a practicum or off-campus experience, who arranges this? Does the graduate school select a site and place you there, or is it your responsibility? What are the professional affiliations of the faculty? Does the program merit any outside professional endorsement or accreditation?

Critically evaluate the catalogs of each of the programs you are considering. List any questions you have and ask current or former teachers and colleagues for their impressions as well.

. . . .

If you are interested in graduate work in public administration, for example, in addition to graduate courses in the areas of your interest—urban planning or management—consider the availability of faculty sharing your interests, directed research opportunities, and specialized seminars.

. . . .

The Application. Preview each application thoroughly to determine what you need to provide in the way of letters of recommendation, transcripts from undergraduate schools or any previous graduate work, and personal essays. Make a notation for each application of what you need to complete that document.

Additionally, you'll want to determine entrance testing requirements for each institution and immediately arrange to complete your test registration. For example, the Graduate Record Exam (GRE) and most professional-school admissions tests have several weeks between the last registration date and the test date. Your local college career office should be able to provide you with test registration booklets, sample test materials, information on test sites and dates, and independent test review materials that might be available commercially.

Visit the Campus if Possible

If time and finances allow, a visit, interview, and tour can help make your decision easier. You can develop a sense of the student body, meet some of the faculty, and hear up-to-date information on resources and the curriculum. You will have a brief opportunity to "try out" the surroundings to see if they fit your needs. After all, it will be home for a while. If a visit is not possible but you have questions, don't hesitate to call and speak with the dean of the graduate school. Most are more than happy to talk to candidates and want them to have the answers they seek. Graduate school admission is a very personal and individual process.

Arrange for Letters of Recommendation

This is also the time to begin to assemble a group of individuals who will support your candidacy as a graduate student by writing letters of recommendation or completing recommendation forms. Some schools will ask you to provide letters of recommendation to be included with your application or sent directly to the school by the recommender. Other graduate programs will provide a recommendation form that must be completed by the recommender. These graduate school forms vary greatly in the amount of space provided for a written recommendation. So that you can use letters as you need to, ask your recommenders to address their letters "To Whom It May Concern," unless one of your recommenders has a particular connection to one of your graduate schools or knows an official at the school.

Choose recommenders who can speak authoritatively about the criteria important to selection officials at your graduate school. In other words, choose recommenders who can write about your grasp of the literature in your field of study, your ability to write and speak effectively, your class performance, and your demonstrated interest in the field outside of class. Other characteristics that graduate schools are interested in assessing include your emotional maturity, leadership ability, breadth of general knowledge, intellectual ability, motivation, perseverance, and ability to engage in independent inquiry.

When requesting recommendations, it's especially helpful to put the request in writing. Explain your graduate school intentions and express some of your thoughts about graduate school and your appreciation for their support. Don't be shy about "prompting" your recommenders with some suggestions of what you would appreciate being included in their comments. Most recommenders will find this direction helpful and will want to produce a statement of support that you can both stand behind. Consequently, if your interaction with one recommender was especially focused on research projects, he or she might be best able to speak of those skills and your critical thinking ability. Another recommender may have good comments to make about your public presentation skills.

Give your recommenders plenty of lead time in which to complete your recommendation, and set a date by which they should respond. If they fail to meet your deadline, be prepared to make a polite call or visit to inquire if they need more information or if there is anything you can do to move the process along.

Whether or not you are providing a graduate school form or asking for an original letter to be mailed, be sure to provide an envelope and postage if the recommender must mail the form or letter directly to the graduate school.

Each recommendation you request should provide a different piece of information about you for the selection committee. It might be pleasant for letters of recommendation to say that you are a fine, upstanding individual, but a selection committee for graduate school will require specific information. Each recommender has had a unique relationship with you, and their letters should reflect that. Think of each letter as helping to build a more complete portrait of you as a potential graduate student.

Write Your Application Statement

. . . .

Many graduate applications for economics programs require a written personal statement. For the economics major, the personal essay should be a welcome opportunity to express your deep interest in pursuing graduate study. Your understanding of the challenges ahead, your commitment to the work involved, and your expressed self-awareness will weigh heavily in the decision process of the graduate school admissions committee.

....

An excellent source to help in thinking about writing this essay is *How to Write a Winning Personal Statement for Graduate and Professional School* by Richard J. Stelzer. It has been written from the perspective of what graduate school selection committees are looking for when they read these essays. It provides helpful tips to keep your essay targeted on the kinds of issues and criteria that are important to selection committees and that provide them with the kind of information they can best utilize in making their decision.

Follow Up on Your Applications

After you have finished each application and mailed it along with your transcript requests and letters of recommendation, be sure to follow up on the progress of your file. For example, call the graduate school administrative staff to see whether your transcripts have arrived. If the school required your recommenders to fill out a specific recommendation form that had to be mailed directly to the school, you will want to ensure that they have all arrived in good time for the processing of your application. It is your responsibility to make certain that all required information is received by the institution.

RESEARCHING FINANCIAL AID SOURCES, SCHOLARSHIPS, AND FELLOWSHIPS

Financial aid information is available from each school, so be sure to request it when you call for a catalog and application materials. There will be several lengthy forms to complete, and these will vary by school, type of school (public versus private), and state. Be sure to note the deadline dates for these important forms.

There are many excellent resources available to help you explore all of your financial aid options. Visit your college career office or local public library to find out about the range of materials available. Two excellent resources include Peterson's *Grants for Graduate Students* and the Foundation Center's *Foundation Grants to Individuals*. These types of resources generally contain information that can be accessed by indexes including field of study, specific eligibility requirements, administering agency, and geographic focus.

EVALUATING ACCEPTANCES

If you apply to and are accepted at more than one school, it is time to return to your initial research and self-assessment to evaluate your options and select the program that will best help you achieve the goals you set for pursuing graduate study. You'll want to choose a program that will allow you to complete your studies in a timely and cost-effective way. This may be a good time to get additional feedback from professors and career professionals who are familiar with your interests and plans. Ultimately, the decision is yours, so be sure you get answers to all the questions you can think of.

SOME NOTES ABOUT REJECTION

Each graduate school is searching for applicants who appear to have the qualifications necessary to succeed in its program. Applications are evaluated on a combination of undergraduate grade point average, strength of letters of recommendation, standardized test scores, and personal statements written for the application.

A carelessly completed application is one reason many applicants are denied admission to a graduate program. To avoid this type of needless rejection, be sure to carefully and completely answer all appropriate questions on the application form, focus your personal statement given the instructions provided, and submit your materials well in advance of the deadline. Remember that your test scores and recommendations are considered a part of your application, so they must also be received by the deadline.

If you are rejected by a school that especially interests you, you may want to contact the dean of graduate studies to discuss the strengths and weaknesses of your application. Information provided by the dean will be useful in reapplying to the program or applying to other, similar programs.

PART TWO

THE CAREER PATHS

CHAPTER NINE

INTRODUCTION TO CAREER PATHS IN ECONOMICS

*E*conomists study the ways society distributes scarce resources such as land, labor, raw materials, and machinery to produce goods and services. They conduct research, collect and analyze data, monitor economic trends, and develop forecasts. They research issues such as energy costs, inflation, interest rates, imports, and employment levels.

Most economists are concerned with practical applications of economic policy in a particular area. They use their understanding of economic relationships to advise businesses and other organizations, including insurance companies, banks, securities firms, industry and trade associations, labor unions, and government agencies.

Economists use mathematical models to develop programs predicting answers to questions such as the nature and length of business cycles, the effects of a specific rate of inflation on the economy, or the effects of tax legislation on unemployment levels. Economists devise methods and procedures for obtaining the data they need. For example, they may use sampling techniques to conduct a survey and various mathematical modeling techniques to develop forecasts.

Preparing reports on research results is an important part of the economist's job. They must review and analyze relevant data, prepare applicable tables and charts, and present the results in clear, concise language that can be understood by noneconomists. Presenting economic and statistical concepts in a meaningful way is particularly important for economists whose research is directed toward making policies for an organization.

WORKING CONDITIONS

Economists usually have structured work schedules. They often work alone, writing reports, preparing statistical charts, and using computers, but they may also be an integral part of a research team. Most work under pressure of deadlines and tight schedules, and sometimes they must work overtime. Their routine may be interrupted by special requests for data, as well as by the need to attend meetings or conferences; regular travel may be necessary to do this.

POSSIBLE JOB TITLES

Listed here are examples of jobs economics majors might choose to pursue upon graduation. Some of them, such as college teaching, require additional education or training beyond the bachelor's degree. And, as you will note, many job titles exist in a variety of sectors. For example, many of the job titles found in the business sector are mirrored in government bodies.

Banking and Financial Services

Accountant	Database administrator
Auditor	Economic forecaster
Bank examiner	Economist
Bank manager	Estate planner
Bank research analyst	Financial adviser
Bond trader	Financial aid director
Commercial credit analyst	Foundation administrator
Commodities broker/stockbroker	Loan counselor
Commodity analyst	Loan officer
Consumer credit manager	Pension funds administrator
Credit accounting coordinator	Portfolio administrator
	Purser

Securities analyst

Securities salesperson/broker

Tax economist

Business

Business manager

Compensation/benefits
administrator

Consumer affairs director

Contract administrator

Cost analyst

Customer account representative

Database administrator

Efficiency expert

Financial economist

Forecaster

Human resources administrator

Industrial economist

Industrial/institutional buyer

Industrial traffic manager

International trade specialist

Management consultant/analyst

Management trainee

Manufacturers representative

Market analyst

Property manager

Purchasing agent

Real estate agent/broker

Researcher

Retail manager

Sales representative

Service representative

Systems evaluator

Technical representative

Wage and salary administrator

Communications

Marketing manager

Marketing research analyst

Publicity specialist

Public relations representative

Consulting

Consultant

Energy

Economic geologist

Government

Budget officer

Cost analyst

Database administrator

Elected official

Foreign service officer

Foreign trade analyst

Government administrator

Information scientist

Intelligence agent

International trade specialist

Labor economist

Lobbyist

Political campaign organizer

Public administrator/manager

Public utilities manager

Regional/urban planner

Social security administrator

Tax administrator

Tax examiner/collector/
revenue agent

Transportation specialist

Treasury management specialist

Urban/regional planner

Health Care

Health care administrator

Health policy planner

Human Services

Corporate trainer

Industrial relations specialist

Labor relations specialist

Personnel manager

Recruiter

Insurance

Actuary

Benefits analyst

Claims adjuster

Database administrator

Demographer

Populations studies analyst

Sales representative

Statistician

Underwriter

Law

Attorney

Judge

Legal assistant

Litigation analyst

Paralegal

Marketing

Database administrator

Marketing manager

Market interviewer

Market research analyst

Market research statistician

Public relations specialist

Teaching

Research assistant

Secondary school teacher

University/college professor

Writing

Editor

Financial reporter

Foreign correspondent

Journalist/columnist

Technical writer

This list is not exhaustive, and through your own research you will, undoubtedly, be able to add to the list substantially.

THE CAREER PATHS

What college student doesn't hope to find a great job upon graduation? With four years of study and careful planning throughout your college program, and in some cases graduate study, there is no reason why, as an economics major, you shouldn't walk into a good job. There are a lot of choices, however, as you see from the list of job titles. The aim of this book is to help you narrow them down and find the career path that best suits your education, interests, and skills.

In this book, we identify and explore five main paths. However, your options are not limited to these five. The following section discusses additional careers that economics majors regularly enter into.

1. Government

2. Marketing

3. Human resources

4. Banking, finance, and investment

5. Teaching

ADDITIONAL PATHS

The five career paths covered in this book are only some of the many paths that economics majors regularly pursue. About one-third of all economists are employed in private industry. They are also hired by manufacturing firms, insurance companies, transportation companies, economic research firms, and management consulting firms. Some additional paths to consider are described next.

Actuarial Careers

Actuaries answer questions about future risk, make pricing decisions, and formulate investment strategies. Some design insurance, financial, and pension plans and ensure that these plans are maintained on a sound financial basis. Most actuaries specialize in life, health, or property and casualty insurance; others specialize in pension plans.

Actuaries assemble and analyze data to estimate probabilities of death, sickness, injury, disability, retirement income level, property loss, or return on investment. They use this information to estimate how much an insurance company will have to pay out in claims, or to make other business decisions. For example, actuaries may calculate the expected amount of claims due to automobile accidents, which can vary depending on the insured's age, sex, driving history, type of car, and other factors. Actuaries ensure that the price charged for such insurance, or premium, will enable the company to cover claims and expenses as they incur. Finally, this premium charged must be profitable and yet be competitive with other insurance companies. The actuary calculates premium rates and determines policy contract provisions for each type of insurance offered.

To perform their duties effectively, actuaries must remain informed about general economic and social trends and legislation, as well as developments in health, business, finance, and economics that may affect insurance or investment practices. Using their broad knowledge of business and mathematics, actuaries may work in investment, risk classification, or pension planning.

Careers in Private Research and Consulting Firms

Many private research and development (R&D) firms, consulting firms, and "think tanks" hire economists. These firms specialize in a wide variety of economic applications. The following are some of the areas covered by these firms:

Cost-benefit analysis

Econometric analysis for firms and government agencies

Environmental studies

Forensic economics (estimating the value of lost income as a result of wrongful injury or death)

International economics

Market research

Higher-level positions in these firms often require a graduate degree in economics. Bachelor's degree holders are often hired as research assistants as the first step.

Health Care Management Careers

Health care is a business, albeit a special one. Like every other business, it needs good management to keep it running smoothly, especially during times of change. The title health services manager encompasses individuals in many different positions who plan, organize, coordinate, and supervise the delivery of health care. Health services managers include both generalists—administrators who manage or help to manage an entire facility or system—and health specialists—managers in charge of specific clinical departments or services found only in the health industry.

The structure and financing of health care is changing rapidly. Future health services managers must be prepared to deal with evolving integrated health care delivery systems, restructuring of work, technological innovations, and an increased focus on preventive care.

Health services managers are called upon to improve efficiency in all health care facilities. Increasingly, health services managers work in organizations in which they must optimize efficiency of a variety of interrelated services, ranging from inpatient care to outpatient follow-up care, for example.

The top administrator or chief executive officer (CEO) and the assistant administrators without specific titles are health care generalists. They set the overall direction of the organization, concentrating on such areas as community outreach, planning, marketing, human resources, finance, and complying with government regulations. Their range of knowledge is broad, including developments in the clinical departments as well as in the business arena.

Insurance Careers

Insurance companies protect individuals and organizations from financial loss by assuming billions of dollars in risks each year. In addition to actuaries, economics majors can become underwriters.

Underwriters identify and analyze the risk of loss from policyholders, establish appropriate premium rates, and write policies that cover that risk. An insurance company may lose business to competitors if the underwriter appraises risks too conservatively, or it may have to pay more claims if the underwriting actions are too liberal.

Technology plays an increasingly important role in an underwriter's job. Underwriters use computer applications called "smart systems" to manage risks more efficiently and accurately. They enter into the computer various information relating to a person or organization whose application for insurance is pending. These systems automatically analyze and rate insurance applications and then recommend acceptance or denial of the risk, or they adjust the premium rate in accordance with the risk. Underwriters are then better equipped to make sound decisions in an effort to avoid excessive losses in the future.

With the aid of computers, underwriters analyze information in insurance applications, reports from loss control consultants, medical reports, and actuarial studies—reports that describe the probability of insured loss. They then decide whether to issue a policy and outline the terms of the contract, including the amount of the premium. Underwriters sometimes correspond with policyholders, agents, and managers about policy cancellations or other matters. On rare occasions, they accompany sales representatives on appointments with prospective clients. (Life insurance agents and brokers are increasingly called life underwriters.)

Most underwriters specialize in one of three major categories of insurance—life, property and casualty, or health. They further specialize in group or individual policies. Property and casualty underwriters often specialize by type of risk insured, such as fire, homeowners', automobile, marine, property, liability, or workers' compensation. In cases where casualty companies insure in a single "package" policy, covering various types of risks, the underwriter must be familiar with different lines of insurance. Some underwriters, called commercial account underwriters, handle business insurance exclusively. They often evaluate a firm's entire operation in appraising its application for insurance.

Careers in Labor and Industrial Relations

Economics majors working in the field of labor and industrial relations are responsible for engaging in contract negotiations, processing labor grievances, and dealing with day-to-day labor-management disputes. (This career path is covered with human resource management careers in Chapter 12.)

Law Careers

Many economics majors use their degree as a stepping stone to entry into law school and a law career. Law schools report that most students who enter law school have two conspicuous deficiencies: (1) the inability to write and/or speak clearly and correctly and (2) the inability to think critically and make valid analytical comparisons and differentiations. Economics is perhaps one of the best disciplines in which students can develop analytical thought with precision and exactness. Law schools are primarily interested in students who possess strong analytical and communication skills and have a solid liberal arts background. An economics degree provides that background. To further build the case for an economics degree as a prelude to law school, a recent study published in the *Journal of Economic Education* showed that economics majors had the highest average LSAT scores among the fourteen majors that had taken the exam in the years studied.

Public Utilities Careers

Economists have been employed by public utilities for a long time. They are called upon to forecast demand, analyze supply, and analyze and interpret industry regulation. With recent changes in the competitive structure of the industry, people with training in economics should be even more in demand.

Public utility economists have a variety of functions, including the following:

Cost analysis

Demand forecasting

Demand-side management

Market analysis

Technology assessment

In addition, economists work in developing and defending a public utility's rate structure.

Transportation Careers

Transportation companies as well as government bodies hire transportation management and economics graduates. The positions available include the following:

Dock supervision

Inventory control

Planning and management of urban and rural transportation systems

Policy analysis

Rate determination

Route development

Scheduling

Transport service marketing

Warehouse and materials management

With a little bit of guidance and creativity, you should be able to make a case for your economics degree in any area you wish to enter.

EMPLOYMENT FIGURES

Economists hold about 52,000 jobs nationwide. Private industry, particularly economic and marketing research firms, management consulting firms, banks, securities and commodities brokers, and computer and data-processing companies, employ about three out of four salaried workers. The remainder of economists are employed by a wide range of government agencies, primarily in state governments. The Departments of Labor, Agriculture, and Commerce are the largest federal employers of economists.

A number of economists combine a full-time job in government, academia, or business with part-time or consulting work in another setting.

Employment of economists is concentrated in large cities. Some economists work abroad for companies with major international operations, for U.S. government agencies such as the Foreign Service, and for international organizations such as the World Bank and the United Nations.

Many economists hold, in addition to the jobs just described, faculty positions in colleges and universities. Economics faculty have flexible work schedules and may divide their time among teaching, research, consulting, and administration.

THE QUALIFICATIONS YOU'LL NEED

Graduate training is required for most private sector economist jobs and for advancement to more responsible positions. Candidates who hold a master's degree in economics have much better employment prospects than bachelor's degree holders.

Economics includes many specialties at the graduate level, such as advanced economic theory, econometrics, international economics, and labor economics. Students should select graduate schools strong in specialties in which they are interested. Some schools help graduate students find internships or part-time employment in government agencies, economic consulting firms, financial institutions, or marketing research firms prior to graduation.

In the federal government, candidates for entry-level economist positions must have a bachelor's degree with a minimum of twenty-one semester hours of economics and three hours of statistics, accounting, or calculus. Competition is keen for positions that require only a bachelor's degree, however. Additional education or superior academic performance is likely to be required to gain employment.

For a job as an instructor in many junior and some community colleges, a master's degree is the minimum requirement. In most colleges and universities, however, a Ph.D. is necessary for appointment as an instructor. A Ph.D. and extensive publications in academic journals are required for a professorship, tenure, and promotion.

Whether working in government, industry, research, marketing, or consulting, economists who have a graduate degree usually qualify for more responsible research and administrative positions. A Ph.D. is necessary for top economist positions in many organizations. Many corporation and government executives have a strong background in economics or marketing.

A bachelor's degree with a major in economics or marketing is generally not sufficient to obtain positions as an economist but is excellent preparation for many entry-level positions as a research assistant, administrative or management trainee, marketing interviewer, or any of a number of professional sales jobs.

Economics majors can choose from a variety of courses, ranging from those that are intensely mathematical, such as microeconomics, macroeconomics, and econometrics, to more philosophical courses, such as the history of economic thought. Because of the importance of quantitative skills to economists, courses in mathematics, statistics, econometrics, sampling theory and survey design, and computer science are extremely helpful.

Aspiring economists should gain experience gathering and analyzing data, conducting interviews or surveys, and writing reports on their findings while in college. This experience can prove invaluable later in obtaining a full-time position in the field, since much of your work, in the beginning, may center around these duties.

With experience, economists eventually are assigned their own research projects. Those considering careers as economists should be able to work accurately because much time is spent on data analysis. Patience and persistence are necessary qualities, since economists must spend long hours on independent study and problem solving.

Economists also must be able to present their findings, both orally and in writing, in a clear, meaningful way.

GRADUATE STUDY

Because so many professional positions in the realm of economics require an advanced degree, economics majors use their bachelor's degree as a stepping stone and go on to study for a master's in areas such as economics, applied mathematics and statistics, public policy, labor relations, law, marketing, international affairs, banking, and public policy. Those preparing for an academic career at the university level usually go on to earn a doctorate.

CAREER OUTLOOK

According to the *Occupational Outlook Handbook*, employment of economists is expected to grow about as fast as the average for all occupations through 2006. Most job openings, however, are likely to result from the need to replace experienced workers who transfer to other occupations, retire, or leave the labor force for other reasons.

Opportunities for economists should be best in private industry, especially in research, testing, and consulting firms, as more companies contract out for economic research services. Competition, the growing complexity of the global economy, and increased reliance on quantitative methods for analyzing the current value of future funds, business trends, sales, and purchasing should spur demand for economists.

The growing need for economic analyses in virtually every industry should result in additional jobs for economists.

Employment of economists in the federal government should decline more slowly than the rate projected for the entire federal workforce. Average employment growth is expected among economists in state and local government.

An advanced degree coupled with a strong background in economic theory, mathematics, statistics, and econometrics provides the basis for acquiring any specialty within the field. Those skilled in quantitative techniques and their application to economic modeling and forecasting coupled with good computer and communications skills should have the best job opportunities.

Those who graduate with a bachelor's degree in economics through 2006 will face keen competition for the limited number of economist positions for which they qualify. You will qualify for a number of other positions, however, where you can take advantage of your economic knowledge in conducting research, developing surveys, or analyzing data. Many graduates with bachelor's degrees will find good jobs in industry and business as management or sales trainees, or administrative assistants. Economists with good quantitative skills are qualified for research assistant positions in a broad range of fields.

Those who meet state certification requirements may become high school economics teachers. The demand for secondary school economics teachers is expected to grow as economics becomes an increasingly important and popular course.

As mentioned earlier, candidates who hold a master's degree in economics have much better employment prospects than bachelor's degree holders. Many businesses, research and consulting firms, and government agencies seek master's degree holders who have strong computer and quantitative skills and can perform complex research but do not command the higher salary of a Ph.D.

Ph.D. degree holders are likely to face significant competition for teaching positions in colleges and universities.

SALARIES

According to a 1997 salary survey by the National Association of Colleges and Employers, graduates with a bachelor's degree in economics received starting salary offers averaging $31,300 a year.

The median base salary of business economists was $73,000, according to a survey by the National Association of Business Economists. The median entry-level salary was about $35,000, with most new entrants possessing a master's degree. In fact, 93 percent of the respondents held advanced degrees. The highest salaries were reported by those who had a Ph.D., with a median salary of $85,000. Master's degree holders earned a median salary of $65,500, while bachelor's degree holders earned $60,000.

The highest paid business economists were in the securities and investment industry, which reported a median income of $100,000, followed by banking and mining at $93,000, and the nondurable manufacturing industry at $87,000. The lowest paid were in government and nonprofit research.

The federal government recognizes education and experience in certifying applicants for entry-level positions. The entrance salary for economists having a bachelor's degree was about $19,500 a year in 1997. Those with superior academic records began at about $24,200. Those with a master's degree qualified for positions at an annual salary of $29,600. Those with a Ph.D. began at $35,800, while some individuals with experience and an advanced degree started at $42,900. Starting salaries were slightly higher in selected areas where the prevailing local pay was higher. The average annual salary for economists employed by the federal government was $63,870 a year in early 1997.

RESOURCES

The Appendices provide additional resources with more information about career paths.

CHAPTER TEN

PATH 1: GOVERNMENT

A bout one quarter of all economists nationwide work for U.S. government agencies, at both the state and federal level.

Economists working in government agencies fill a variety of roles and work in almost every area of government. They may assess economic conditions in the United States or abroad to estimate the economic effects of specific changes in legislation or public policy. Or they may study issues such as how the dollar's fluctuation against foreign currencies affects import and export levels.

The majority of government economists work in the area of agriculture, labor, or quantitative analysis. Some economists in the U.S. Department of Commerce study production, distribution, and consumption of commodities produced overseas, while economists employed with the Bureau of Labor Statistics analyze data on the domestic economy: prices, wages, employment, productivity, and safety and health. An economist working in state or local government might analyze data on the growth of school-aged populations, prison growth, and employment and unemployment rates to project spending needs for future years.

POSSIBLE GOVERNMENT SETTINGS

Economists work for government agencies, departments, and programs such as the following:

Bureau of Labor Statistics

Bureau of the Census

Commerce Department

Congressional Budget Office

Consumer Product Safety
Commission

Department of Agriculture

Department of Commerce

Department of Energy

Department of Health and
Human Services

Department of Housing and
Urban Development

Department of Labor

Department of State

Department of the Interior

Department of the Treasury

Environmental Protection Agency

Federal Reserve Board

Foreign Service (Department
of State)

National Credit Union
Administration

National Labor Relations Board

Office of Management and Budget

Office of the Comptroller of the
Currency

Peace Corps

Pension Benefit Guaranty
Corporation

Securities and Exchange Commission

Selective Service System

Small Business Administration

Social Security Administration

United States Information Agency

United States International
Development Cooperation Agency

United States International
Trade Commission

This list is by no means exhaustive. Through your own investigation, you will probably be able to add many more agencies and departments to the list.

POSSIBLE JOB TITLES

The U.S. Government has assigned a number of job titles based on college major. The following job titles fall into the realm of employment an economics major could be qualified for. Related majors and their associated job titles are also included here. You will find some of the same job titles assigned to several majors.

Major: Economics

Actuary

Budget analyst

Contract specialist

Economist

Financial analyst

Financial institution examiner

General Accounting Office (GAO) evaluator

Loan specialist

Trade specialist

Transportation industrial analyst

Major: Employee/Labor Relations

Contractor industrial relations specialist

Employee relations specialist

Hearing and appeals specialist

Labor management relations examiner

Labor relations specialist

Mediator

Salary and wage administrator

Workers' compensation claims examiner

Major: Finance

Appraiser and assessor

Budget analyst

Financial administrator

Financial analyst

Financial institution examiner

Securities compliance examiner

Tax examiner

Trade specialist

Major: Hospital Administration

Administrative officer

General health scientist

Health system administrator

Health system specialist

Hospital housekeeper

Miscellaneous administration and programs specialist

Public health programs specialist

Major: Human Resource Management

Apprenticeship and training representative

Employee development specialist

Equal employment opportunity specialist

Military personnel management specialist

Personnel manager

Position classification specialist

Major: Insurance

Crop insurance administrator

Miscellaneous administration and programs specialist

Program analyst

Social insurance administrator

Social insurance claims examiner

Unemployment insurance specialist

Major: International Relations

Foreign affairs specialist

Foreign agriculture affairs specialist

Intelligence specialist

International relations worker

Language specialist

Public affairs specialist

Trade specialist

Major: Law

Administrative law judge

Attorney

GAO evaluator

Hearing and appeals specialist

Legal instruments examiner

Paralegal specialist

Patent attorney

Tax law specialist

Major: Marketing

Agriculture marketing specialist

Bond sales promotion representative

Business and industry specialist

Contract specialist

Inventory management specialist

Packaging specialist

Property disposal specialist

Supply specialist

Trade specialist

Major: Mathematics

Actuary

Cartographer

Computer science specialist

Mathematician

Mathematical statistician

Operations research analyst

Statistician

Major: Planning, Community or City

Community planner

Realtor

Major: Political Science/Government

Archivist

Budget analyst

GAO evaluator

Historian

Foreign affairs specialist

Miscellaneous administration and programs specialist

Program analyst

Public affairs specialist

Social scientist

Major: Public Administration

Budget analyst

Employee development specialist

Employee relations specialist

GAO evaluator

Housing manager

Management analyst

Manpower development specialist

Miscellaneous administration and programs specialist

Program analyst

Public utilities specialist

Major: Public Relations

Contact representative

Foreign affairs specialist

Foreign agriculture affairs specialist

Public affairs specialist

Major: Statistics

Actuary

Computer science specialist

Mathematical statistician

Operations research analyst

Program analyst

Statistician

Transportation industry analyst

Any Major

Administrative officer

Air traffic controller

Civil rights analyst

Claims examiner

Contract administrator

Contract representative

Editor

Environmental protection agent

General investigator

Internal revenue officer

Logistics manager

Management analyst

Paralegal specialist

Personnel occupations officer

THE QUALIFICATIONS YOU'LL NEED

Landing a higher-level government position often requires a graduate degree in economics. Graduates with a bachelor's degree are generally hired as research or economics assistants as the initial appointment. Advancement comes over time.

Students interested in pursuing a career in government service should try to include the following courses in their undergraduate curriculum: mathematical economics; law and economics; econometrics; economics of regulation; and forecasting.

It is also important to acquire experience with database and statistical software, and strong communication skills are essential.

FINDING YOUR GOVERNMENT JOB

The very best way these days to find a job in the U.S. government is to take advantage of the new system the government has created for just this purpose. Forget what you have heard about the complexities of finding a federal job. Your job search and application is now a simple three-step process.

Although the actual job search is your responsibility, the U.S. Office of Personnel Management (OPM) has developed the USAJOBS system to assist you along the way. By using USAJOBS, you have access to federal job listings, some state and local government listings, as well as private sector listings. USAJOBS provides current information, updated daily, and is available twenty-four hours a day, seven days a week.

Step 1: Use Any of the Automated Components of the Federal Employment Information System

USAJOBS, the federal government's employment information system, has easily accessible federal employment information. USAJOBS provides worldwide job vacancy information, employment information fact sheets, and job applications and forms. It also has on-line resume development and electronic transmission capabilities. In many instances, job seekers can apply for positions on-line.

USAJOBS is updated every business day from a database of more than 7,500 worldwide job opportunities. USAJOBS is available to job seekers in a variety of formats, ensuring access for customers with differing physical and technological capabilities. It is accessible through the computer or telephone.

USAJOBS consists of the following components:

Internet. The official worldwide website for jobs and employment information may be accessed at http://www.usajobs.opm.gov. On the website, job seekers can access worldwide current job vacancies, employment information fact sheets, and applications and forms. And, in some instances, job seekers can apply for jobs on-line.

Complete job announcements can be retrieved from the website. The USAJOBS website also has an on-line resume builder feature. Using the resume builder, job seekers can create on-line resumes specifically designed for applying for federal jobs. Resumes created on the USAJOBS resume builder can be printed from the system for faxing or mailing to employers and saved and edited for future use. For many of the vacancies listed on the site, job seekers can submit resumes created through USAJOBS directly to hiring agencies through an electronic submission process.

The U.S. Office of Personnel Management (OPM) also provides current employment information through the Federal Job Opportunities Board (FJOB) at (912) 757-3100. This is an electronic bulletin board, so you need a personal computer equipped with a modem and communications software, as well as a telephone line. The FJOB can also be accessed through the Internet via Telnet at fjob.opm.gov.

Touch Screen Computer Kiosk. A kiosk network of self-service information providers is located in OPM offices and many federal buildings nationwide. At the touch of a finger, job seekers can access worldwide current job vacancies, employment information fact sheets, and applications and forms. Complete job announcements can be retrieved from the kiosk.

Automated Telephone System. You can reach an interactive voice response telephone system at (912) 757-3000 or TDD (912) 744-2299, or in person at seventeen OPM service centers located throughout the country (local numbers are listed in the blue pages). By telephone, job seekers can access worldwide current job vacancies, employment information fact sheets, and applications and forms, as well as, in some instances, apply for jobs. Federal agencies list job opportunities on the federal employment information system. The system is accessible from a number of user-friendly mediums.

Step 2: Obtain the Vacancy Announcement

Once you have found an opportunity that interests you, you will need more information on the specific opportunity and appropriate application forms. Use USAJOBS to obtain a copy of the vacancy announcement. The vacancy announcement is an important source of information. Most of the questions you are likely to have will be answered as you read through the announcement.

Vacancy announcements include closing/deadline dates for applications, specific duties of the position, whether or not a written test is required, educational requirements, duty location, salary, as well as other details.

Step 3: Follow the Application Instructions

You may apply for most jobs with a resume, the Optional Application for Federal Employment (OF-612), or any written format you choose. For jobs that are unique or filled through automated procedures, you may be given special forms and/or instructions in the job announcement. Although the federal government does not require a standard application form for most jobs, certain information is needed to evaluate your qualifications. If you decide to submit any format other than the OF-612 (i.e., a resume), you must include the following information:

Job Information. Include the announcement number, title, and grade.

Personal Information. Include your full name, mailing address (with zip code), day and evening phone numbers (with area code), social security number, country of citizenship, veterans' preference, reinstatement eligibility, and highest federal civilian grade held.

Education. Include your high school's name, city, and state, and the names of colleges or universities you've attended, including their city and state. Also list your major and types of degrees received and in what year. (If you don't have a degree, show your total credits earned and indicate whether they are semester or quarter hours.)

Work Experience. Include your job titles, duties and accomplishments, employers' names and addresses, supervisors' names and phone numbers, starting and ending dates (month and year), hours per week, salary, and whether or not your current supervisor may be contacted. Prepare a separate entry for each job.

Other Qualifications. Include job-related training courses (title and year), job-related skills, job-related certificates and licenses, and job-related honors, awards, and special accomplishments.

FEDERAL EMPLOYMENT OVERSEAS

The federal government has technical, administrative, and supervisory employment opportunities overseas. These positions are usually in the competitive federal service and, as vacancies occur, are typically filled by transferring career federal employees from the United States. Only when federal employees are not available for transfer overseas, and qualified United States citizens cannot be recruited locally, are these vacancies filled through the open examination process. For opportunities overseas, see detailed information at http://www.usajobs.opm.gov/b1b.htm.

Individuals may also apply directly to federal agencies for excepted service positions such as attaché office clerk-translator, translator, interpreter, and Foreign Service, Department of State positions.

Federal employers of individuals overseas include, but are not limited to, the following agencies:

Agency for International Development

Department of Agriculture

Department of Commerce

Department of Defense

Department of State

Department of the Air Force

Department of the Army

Department of the Navy

Peace Corps

U.S. Information Agency

Qualifications for U.S. Government Jobs Overseas

Generally, the qualification requirements for overseas jobs are the same as those established for positions in the United States. Applicants may, however, be required to meet certain additional or higher standards. For example, a foreign language capability, while not required in all federal jobs overseas, would obviously be a valuable qualification.

STUDENT PROGRAMS WITH THE FEDERAL GOVERNMENT

The federal government is interested in finding people from diverse backgrounds who have the skills needed to meet its future employment needs. While some federal agencies have developed agency-specific programs and seek students in specific majors, such as economics, there are also a variety of internships, work-study opportunities, cooperative education appointments, and summer programs that can lead to hiring in all federal agencies. Full information is available at http://www.usajobs.opm.gov/ei13.htm.

GOVERNMENT SALARIES

For 1999 (the latest figures available), the basic pay under the government's General Schedule (GS) pay plan is as follows:

GS-1	$13,362	GS-6	$22,948	GS-11	$37,744
GS-2	$15,023	GS-7	$25,501	GS-12	$45,236
GS-3	$16,392	GS-8	$28,242	GS-13	$53,793
GS-4	$18,401	GS-9	$31,195	GS-14	$63,567
GS-5	$20,588	GS-10	$34,353	GS-15	$74,773

GS pay is adjusted geographically, and the majority of jobs pay a higher salary than those listed here. When locality payments are included, pay rates in the continental United States are 5.6 percent to 12 percent higher. Pay rates outside the continental United States are 10 percent to 25 percent higher. Where warranted by conditions at the post, employees may receive a post differential or cost-of-living allowance.

Also, certain hard-to-fill jobs, usually in the scientific, technical, or medical fields, may have higher starting salaries. Exact pay information can be found on position vacancy announcements.

SAMPLE JOB ANNOUNCEMENTS

To get an idea of the kind of positions available and the salaries they command, examine the sample job announcements in Exhibits 10.1 through 10.3. (Contact information is not provided here because these particular positions will have already been filled.)

Exhibit 10.1

Economist Announcement (1)

Position: Economist

Salary: GS-7 = $26,263 to $34,137 annually

Promotion Potential: GS-11

Hiring Agency: Department of Labor, Bureau of Labor Statistics

Duty Location: Atlanta, Georgia

Conditions of Employment: Candidates for this position must travel 80 to 85 percent of the time.

Recruitment Bonuses: For this position, a recruitment bonus of $4,000 will be offered to Outstanding Scholar candidates—college graduates who obtained a 3.45 or higher grade point average on a 4.0 scale for all undergraduate courses or who graduated in the upper 10 percent of their class or major university or college subdivision.

Description of Duties: Positions are advanced developmental level (GS-7), which are preparatory for higher level work as economists. Incumbents gain the expertise required to perform data collection and technical work in the field of compensation, working conditions, or price indexes. Duties include investigating and evaluating data, initiating contacts, preparing technical reports, and providing assistance to survey respondents.

Basic Qualification Requirements: Candidates for economist must have: (1) completed a bachelor's degree in economics that included at least twenty-one semester hours in economics and three semester hours in statistics, accounting, or calculus, or (2) have a combination of education and experience, including courses equivalent to a major in economics, as described in 1 above, plus appropriate experience or additional education.

Additional Qualification Requirements: In addition to meeting the Basic Qualification Requirements, the GS-7 candidate must also have: (1) one year of graduate-level education (eighteen semester hours or equivalent) in

continued

continued

economics; (2) Superior Academic Achievement at the undergraduate level; (3) one year of specialized experience comparable to the GS-5 level in federal service (specialized experience is defined as experience evaluating adequacy of economic reporting requirements and collecting economic data in the areas of price indexes, compensation, and so on); or (4) a combination of graduate level education and specialized experience as described in 1 and 2 above, which, when combined, equals 100 percent of the total specialized experience for this position. (Note: Only graduate education beyond the first nine semester hours or equivalent may be combined with specialized experience.)

Superior Academic Achievement (SAA) is based on either (1) class standing, (2) grade point average (GPA), or (3) honor society membership.

1. Class Standing: Applicants must be in the upper third of the graduating class in the college, university, or major subdivision, such as the College of Liberal Arts or the School of Business Administration, based on completed courses.

2. GPA: Applicants must have a GPA (4.0 scale) of (1) 3.0 or higher as recorded on their official transcript, as computed based on four years of education, or as computed based on courses completed during the final two years of the curriculum, or (2) 3.5 or higher based on the average of the required courses completed in the major field or the required courses in the major field completed during the final two years of the curriculum.

3. National Scholastic Honor Society: Applicants should be elected to membership in a national scholastic honor society.

Exhibit 10.2

Economist Announcement (2)

Position: Economist

Series/Grade: GS-11/12

Salary: $41,262 to $64,289 annually

Promotion Potential: GS-12

Hiring Agency: Department of Commerce, Bureau of the Census

Duty Location: Boston, Massachusetts

Duties: The incumbent performs economic analysis and/or research relative to the program(s) of the organization to which assigned. Works with the Research Data Center (RDC) Partner (National Bureau of Economic Research [NBER]) and the Boston Regional Office (BRO) to maintain a secure computing environment, according to approved Census Bureau procedures. Maintains secure custody of all confidential data at the RDC office. Supervises and monitors any merging of Census Bureau data with external data that researchers bring into the RDC office as part of their projects. In consultation and coordination with Center of Economic Studies (CES) headquarters staff, performs disclosure analysis on any research output the researchers wish to remove from the RDC. Carries out extracts of data for researchers' projects from data sets that the Census Bureau authorizes to reside at the RDC. Provides consultation on use of the data and acts as a liaison to experts on data at CES or other parts of the Census Bureau. Works closely with the RDC Partner and CES management to administer the RDC. Coordinates the review process for research proposals submitted to the RDC; writes or participates in writing documents such as contracts, renewals of the underlying Memorandum of Understanding for the RDC, financial or activity reports, and annual reports; and represents the Census Bureau on the RDC Project Review Board. Carries out research projects.

Qualifications Required: Applicants must have a bachelor's degree in economics that was obtained from an accredited college or university and that included at

continued

continued

least twenty-one semester hours in economics and three semester hours in statistics, accounting, or calculus; OR a combination of education and experience with course work equivalent to a major in economics (as explained above), plus appropriate experience or additional education. For the GS-11, applicants must have three full years of progressively higher-level graduate education or Ph.D. or equivalent doctoral degree OR one year equivalent to at least GS-9 level in the federal service. For the GS-12, applicants must have one year of specialized experience equivalent to the GS-11 level in the federal service. Specialized experience must have equipped the applicant with the particular knowledge, skills, and abilities necessary to successfully perform the duties of the position and that is typically in or related to the work of the position to be filled.

Exhibit 10.3

Economist Announcement (3)

Position: Economist, industrial

Series/Grade: GS-12/13

Salary: GS-12: $48,796 to $63,436 annually
GS-13: $58,027 to $75,433 annually

Promotion Potential: GS-13

Hiring Agency: Department of Transportation (DOT), Surface Transportation Board

Duty Location: Washington, D.C.

Duties: The incumbent conducts economic special studies, analyses, and investigations related to the Board's regulation of the rail transportation industry. He or she analyzes and evaluates the economic impact of actual or proposed legislation; supports the Board's efforts in its regulation of transportation; provides expert economic and analytical advice to the Board staff or officials on industry matters of regulatory concern in the transportation industry; and develops and maintains contacts within the Board, other government agencies, private industry, and with professional economists to keep abreast of economic, industry, and related developments to ensure the Board is provided with current policy guidance.

Basic Qualification Requirements: Applicants for all grade levels must meet one of the following basic requirements: (1) have completed a four-year course of study leading to a bachelor's degree in economics that included at least twenty-one semester hours in economics and three semester hours in statistics, accounting, or calculus, or (2) have a combination of undergraduate level education and experience that totals four years (forty-eight months). Education course work must have included at least twenty-one semester hours in economics and three semester hours in statistics, accounting, or calculus. Experience must have included performing duties such as interpreting economic data or financial indicators; conducting cost/benefit or cost-effectiveness studies; conducting economic research or coordinating economic projects requiring evaluation and interpretation of economic information; or teaching assignments in a college or university that involved class instruction and (1) personal research, (2) direction of graduate theses in economics, or (3) consultant or adviser service on technical economics problems.

Mandatory Qualification Requirements:

1. Knowledge of the Windows operating system for personal computers.

2. Knowledge of personal computer software for word processing (e.g., WordPerfect or MS Word), electronic spreadsheets (e.g., Excel or Lotus 1-2-3), and database management (e.g., MS Access or Paradox).

Additional Qualification Requirements: In addition to the Basic and Mandatory Qualification Requirements stated above, to qualify for GS-12/13 level positions, your experience must also include one year (fifty-two weeks) of experience performing duties such as conducting economic studies, analyses, and investigations and analyzing and evaluating the economic impact of actual or proposed regulations.

FOREIGN SERVICE

A career serving your country overseas can offer excitement, challenge, and even glamour. As a member of the Foreign Service, which is under the jurisdiction of the United States Department of State, you can travel the world and, at the same time, gain the satisfaction of helping other people and representing the interests of your country.

Being a part of the Foreign Service is more than just a job. It is a complete way of life that requires dedication and commitment. If you're smart enough and tough enough to get the job done, the Foreign Service might just be the right place for you.

Different Positions Within the Foreign Service

The Foreign Service divides the different specialty areas into the following "cones":

Administration. Administrative personnel at overseas posts are responsible for hiring foreign national workers, providing office and residential space, assuring reliable communications with Washington, D.C., supervising computer systems, and—of great importance in hostile or unfriendly areas—providing security for the post's personnel and property.

Consular Services. Consular workers must often combine the skills of lawyers, judges, investigators, and social workers. Their duties range from issuing passports and visas to finding a lost child or helping a traveler in trouble.

Economic Officers. Economic officers maintain contact with key business and financial leaders in the host country and report to Washington on the local economic conditions and their impact on American trade and investment policies. They are concerned with issues such as commercial aviation safety, fishing rights, and international banking.

Political Affairs. Those working in political affairs analyze and report on the political views of the host country. They make contact with labor unions, humanitarian organizations, educators, and cultural leaders.

Information and Cultural Affairs. As part of the Foreign Service, the United States Information Agency (USIA) promotes U.S. cultural, informational, and public diplomacy programs. An information officer might develop a library open to the public, meet with the press, and oversee English-language training programs for the host country.

Commercial and Business Services. In this division, a Foreign Service officer identifies overseas business connections for American exporters and investors, conducts market research for the success of U.S. products, and organizes trade shows and other promotional events.

Foreign Service officers can be based in Washington, D.C., or can be sent anywhere in the world. They work at embassies, consulates, and other diplomatic missions in major cities or small towns. They help the thousands of Americans traveling and living overseas, issue visas to citizens of other countries wishing to visit the United States, and help our government execute its foreign policies.

The Foreign Service officer accepts direction from the president of the United States and his top appointees. The main goal is to make U.S. policies succeed. He or she is expected to place loyalty over personal opinions and preferences.

Foreign Service workers can experience a glamorous lifestyle, dining with their ambassador in a European palace, meeting royalty or other heads of state. They can be present at important decision-making sessions and influence world politics and history. But postings can offer hardship as well, in environments as hostile as Antarctica or a Middle Eastern desert. Some assignments, or postings, are in isolated locations without all the familiar comforts of home. The weather can be harsh, and there can be health hazards. Danger from unrest or war is always possible.

In spite of the difficulties, those in the Foreign Service are usually happy with the unique rewards and opportunities.

Training. Although many Foreign Service officers are skilled in political science and history, these days candidates can have knowledge in specialized fields such as the environment, computer science, the fight against AIDS, antidrug efforts, and trade.

There are several steps to complete in order to apply for a position in the Foreign Service:

Written Examination. This is a daylong multiple-choice test usually given once a year. It measures verbal and numerical reasoning, political and cultural awareness, English-language expression, and knowledge of topics important to the function of the Foreign Service. It's a difficult exam, and many people have to take it more than once before they pass.

Oral Evaluation. Those who pass the written exam will be invited to participate in an all-day oral assessment. It tests the skills, abilities, knowledge, and personal characteristics necessary to succeed in the Foreign Service. Writing skills are also measured, as well as administrative, problem-solving, leadership, and interpersonal skills.

Medical Clearance. Because many postings have inadequate health care or pose health hazards, candidates for the Foreign Service must meet a high medical standard. Allowances are made, however, for certain handicaps.

Background Investigation. The Department of State, along with other federal, state, and local agencies, conducts a thorough background check on Foreign Service candidates. They examine employment records, credit history, repayment of school loans, drug abuse, and criminal records.

Eligibility

Before you can take the Foreign Service written examination you must be

- at least twenty years old on the date of the exam
- no more than fifty-nine years old
- a citizen of the United States
- available for worldwide assignment

Job Outlook. The Foreign Service exam is not always offered on a yearly basis—the exam is given when there are definite positions to fill. Because competition is keen for all positions, the number of candidates tends to always exceed the number of openings. Most openings arise from the need to replace Foreign Service workers who retire or leave the profession for other reasons.

Salaries

The starting salary is generally low, but it may be increased at overseas posts with free housing, furniture and utilities, travel expenses, educational allowances for children, and cost-of-living allowances in high-cost cities. Extra pay is also given for dangerous and "hardship" posts.

CLOSE-UP

JIM VAN LANINGHAM, GENERAL SERVICES OFFICER

Jim Van Laningham has made the Foreign Service his career for more than fifteen years. He's been posted in Russia in the former Soviet Union, and in Poland, Morocco, Iraq, and Washington, D.C. He is a General Service officer, which falls under the administration cone.

Getting Started

"Originally, I became interested about the time I was in junior high school. I had just read the book *The Ugly American*, and it talked about the image of Americans overseas and how Foreign Service officers helped correct what often was a bad image. It got me thinking about it. Eventually I took the Foreign Service exam, and I got in.

"I earned a bachelor's degree in economics; then went on for a master's in international business. I took the exam right after I graduated and all the information was still fresh. My education was very helpful.

"It was a year and a half from the time I took the exam until I got accepted. I was very excited. They called me up one day and asked if I could be there in less than a month. They wanted an answer right away. My wife and I discussed it and decided to take the plunge. We went to Washington and they gave me about two months of training in a basic orientation course for new officers and six months of language training.

"After that, I was assigned to the embassy in Moscow as an economics officer. But today it's almost mandatory that the first tour for most Foreign Service officers is as a consular officer, issuing visas to people who want to come to the United States."

What the Work Is Like

"An administrative officer is the person responsible for keeping the embassy operating on a day-to-day basis. First thing in the morning I might find a series of cables from Washington waiting for me, which would require me to report on certain information. Depending on the time of the year, I may be involved in renewing leases on houses we rent for our American staff, or I may be involved in preparing the budget for the embassy, which could be anywhere from a million dollars and up. The budget covers salaries of embassy staff, electricity and other utilities, and procurement of paper and pencils and computers and copy machines and other office equipment.

"For lunch, I may meet with several of my counterparts from other embassies, administrative officers from Australia or Canada or Great Britain, to discuss issues.

continued

continued

"Later on in the day, I may be involved in some personnel issues where I evaluate employee performance and recommend promotion. Or I may have a discipline problem with an employee and have to talk to him about it. I'm even responsible for having to fire someone if necessary.

"Entertaining is a big part of a Foreign Service officer's life—either having local people or people from other embassies to dinner or going to dinner at someone else's house. Oftentimes, you learn a lot about what's going on in the country from talking to other diplomats or the people who live there.

"On weekends, you can travel around the country, go to other cities and see what there is to see—not only just to play tourist, but to meet other people and talk to them.

"What I like most about being an administrative officer in the Foreign Service is the opportunity to see a problem, determine what the solution is, and then see it through to the end. Obviously, travel is also a very attractive part of the job. You can live overseas in a country for a number of years and really get to know what it's like in depth.

"And, for me, there's a lot of excitement about being able to represent the United States overseas. Meeting important people in the country where you are living and perhaps even affecting how relations develop between the United States and that country.

"I was posted in Iraq at the time Saddam Hussein invaded Kuwait. I had been scheduled to fly home to attend my high school reunion, but, of course, there were no planes leaving the country and I couldn't get out.

"We were able to evacuate most of the staff of the American embassy in Baghdad, and then we had about one hundred people from the embassy in Kuwait who were trying to get back to the United States. Although, originally, we were given permission for them to leave, it turned out they were not able to. A lot of my time for about three days was spent trying to get exit visas. The permission finally came through at about three o'clock in the morning, Iraqi time.

"I suddenly remembered that was the exact time my high school reunion had been scheduled. I knew the telephone number where the reunion was being held, so I called and ended up talking to about forty of my former classmates over the phone. Between that and having just succeeded in getting visas for a hundred people to get out of the country, it made a wonderful experience, one that I won't quickly forget.

"Another benefit working with the Foreign Service is that you can retire at age fifty with twenty years of service.

"There are always some downsides, however. When you have a very large organization like the State Department, and you have a lot of different officers with various interests, and you're working on a problem where it's necessary to get the approval of all those officers on any action you want to take, it can be time-consuming and frustrating.

"And as the U.S. government faces a shrinking budget and the State Department faces a shrinking budget, there's less money to get things accomplished with.

"But as frustrating as it can be at times, it's a fabulous career. There's no such thing as a regular routine, and every day you can have a new challenge in front of you. For me, it's a fun way of life."

Advice from Jim Van Laningham

"You have to be able to write well, to organize thoughts logically and coherently. You have to be outgoing because you deal with a lot of different people and you have to have people skills. I think you have to be interested in the world and what's going on around you, because a lot of what you do is reporting back to Washington on what's happening in the country you're in.

"And if you're in the administration cone, hopefully you are a good manager of people. You have to have leadership ability. It also helps to be familiar with finances and budgets.

"But I don't think there's any one particular field of study that leads to the Foreign Service. The people I've met have taken every imaginable major in school. It's more just studying well and doing well and getting a well-rounded education."

RESOURCES

The Federal Web Locator

The Federal Web Locator is a service provided by the Center for Information Law and Policy and is intended to be the one-stop-shopping point for federal government information on the World Wide Web. This list is maintained to bring the cyber citizen to the federal government's doorstep. You can find it on the Web at http://www.law.vill.edu/fed-agency/fedwebloc.html.

Search the following sources for job titles such as economist, research assistant, and economics assistant.

Fedworld's listing of Federal Government Jobs at
http://www.fedworld.gov/categor.htm.

U.S. Office of Personnel Management list of job openings at
http://www.usajobs.opm.gov/b4.htm.

Federal Pay Schedules at http://www.opm.gov/oca/payrates/index.htm.

Foreign Service Information

Contact the Department of State at the following address:

Department of State
Recruitment Division
P.O. Box 9317
Rosslyn Station
Arlington, VA 22209
1-800-JOB-OVERSEAS

CHAPTER ELEVEN

PATH 2: MARKETING

Within the broad field of marketing there are several areas that would be of interest to economics majors. These branches carry job titles such as marketing research analyst, marketing manager, sales manager, and public relations manager.

DEFINITION OF THE CAREER PATHS

Marketing Research Analyst

Marketing research analysts are concerned with the potential sales of a product or service. They analyze statistical data on past sales to predict future sales. They gather data on competitors and analyze prices, sales, and methods of marketing and distribution.

Marketing research analysts do research to find out how well products or services are received by the market. This may include the planning, implementation, and analysis of surveys to determine people's needs and preferences.

Like economists, marketing research analysts devise methods and procedures for obtaining the data they need. They often design telephone, personal, or mail interview surveys to assess consumer preferences. The surveys are usually conducted by trained interviewers under the marketing research analyst's direction. Once the data are compiled, marketing research analysts evaluate it. They then make recommendations to their client or employer based upon their findings. They provide a company's management with information needed to make decisions on the promotion, distribution, design, and pricing of company products or services, or to determine the advisability of adding new lines of merchandise, opening new branches, or otherwise diversifying the company's operations.

Analysts also may conduct opinion research to determine public attitudes on various issues. This can help political or business leaders assess public support for their electoral prospects or advertising policies.

Market research firms use econometric and statistical techniques to forecast the demand for alternative products. These firms conduct and analyze survey data to estimate the potential market for new or revised products. Some of the higher-quality market research firms use sophisticated econometric techniques to estimate the own-price, cross-price, and income elasticities of demands for alternative products. Census data is also used to examine the demographic structure of alternative geographical markets.

Marketing Manager

The executive vice president for marketing in large firms directs the overall marketing policy, including market research, marketing strategy, sales, advertising, promotion, pricing, product development, and public relations activities. These activities are supervised by middle and supervisory managers who oversee staffs of professionals and technicians.

Marketing managers develop the firm's detailed marketing strategy. With the help of staff, including product development managers and market research managers, they determine the demand for products and services offered by the firm and its competitors and identify potential consumers, such as business firms, wholesalers, retailers, government, or the general public. Mass markets are further categorized according to various factors such as region, age, income, and lifestyle.

Marketing managers develop pricing strategy with an eye toward maximizing the firm's share of the market and its profits while ensuring that the firm's customers are satisfied. In collaboration with sales, product development, and other managers, they monitor trends that indicate the need for new products and services and oversee product development.

Marketing managers work with advertising and promotion managers to best promote the firm's products and services and to attract potential users.

Sales Manager

Sales managers direct the firm's sales program. They assign sales territories and goals and establish training programs for their sales representatives. Managers advise their sales representatives on ways to improve their sales performance. In large, multiproduct firms, they oversee regional and local sales managers and their staffs. Sales managers maintain contact with dealers and distributors. They analyze sales statistics gathered by their staffs to determine sales potential and inventory requirements and monitor the preferences of customers. Such information is vital to develop products and maximize profits.

Public Relations Manager

Public relations managers direct publicity programs to a targeted public. They use any necessary communication media in their effort to maintain the support of the specific group upon whom their organization's success depends, such as consumers, stockholders, or the general public. For example, public relations managers may clarify or justify the firm's point of view on health or environmental issues to community or special interest groups. They may evaluate advertising and promotion programs for compatibility with public relations efforts.

Public relations managers, in effect, serve as the eyes and ears of top management. They observe social, economic, and political trends that might ultimately have an effect upon the firm, and they make recommendations to enhance the firm's public image in view of those trends. Public relations managers may confer with labor relations managers to produce internal company communications, such as news about employee-management relations, and with financial managers to produce company reports. They may assist company executives in drafting speeches, arranging interviews, and other forms of public contact; oversee company archives; and respond to information requests. In addition, public relations managers may handle special events, such as sponsorship of races, parties introducing new products, or other activities the firm supports in order to gain public attention through the press without advertising directly.

POSSIBLE JOB SETTINGS

Market research analysts, marketing managers, sales managers, and public relations specialists find employment in a variety of settings, including government agencies, manufacturers, economic consulting firms, financial institutions, research and development consulting firms, marketing research firms, motor vehicle dealers, printing and publishing firms, advertising agencies, department stores, computer and data-processing services firms, and management and public relations firms.

WORKING CONDITIONS

Marketing Research Analyst

Like economists, marketing research analysts have structured work schedules, often working alone, writing reports, preparing statistical charts, and using computers. But some job settings require the marketing research analyst to work as a part of a research team.

The work involves pressure of deadlines and tight schedules, and often there are overtime hours involved.

Marketing, Sales, and Public Relations Manager

Marketing, sales, and public relations managers are provided with offices close to top managers. Long hours, including evenings and weekends, are common. Working under pressure is unavoidable as schedules change, problems arise, and deadlines and goals must be met.

Marketing, advertising, and public relations managers meet frequently with other managers; some meet with the public and government officials. Substantial travel may be involved. For example, attendance at meetings sponsored by associations or industries is often mandatory. Sales managers travel to national, regional, and local offices and to various dealers and distributors. Advertising and promotion managers may travel to meet with clients or representatives of communications media. Public relations managers may travel to meet with special-interest groups or government officials. Job transfers between headquarters and regional offices are common, particularly among sales managers, and may disrupt family life.

THE QUALIFICATIONS YOU'LL NEED

Marketing Research Analyst

Whether working in government, industry, research organizations, marketing, or consulting firms, economists and marketing research analysts who have a graduate degree usually qualify for more responsible research and administrative positions. A Ph.D. is necessary for top economist or marketing positions in many organizations. Many corporation and government executives have a strong background in economics or marketing.

Graduate training is required for most private sector marketing research analyst jobs and for advancement to more responsible positions. Marketing research analysts may earn advanced degrees in economics, business administration, marketing, statistics, or some closely related discipline.

Experience is an important plus to add to your resume. Some schools help graduate students find internships or part-time employment in government agencies, economic consulting firms, financial institutions, or marketing research firms prior to graduation.

A bachelor's degree with a major in economics or marketing is generally not sufficient to obtain a position as a marketing analyst but is excellent preparation for many entry-level positions, including research assistant, administrative or management trainee, marketing interviewer, or any of a number of professional sales jobs.

Aspiring marketing research analysts should gain experience gathering and analyzing data, conducting interviews or surveys, and writing reports on their findings while in college. This experience can prove invaluable later in obtaining a full-time position in the field, since much of their work, in the beginning, may center around these duties. Experience with database, spreadsheet, and statistical software is also very important.

Strong communications skills are also essential for positions of this sort. Students interested in this type of career are encouraged to develop strong skills in both written and oral communication.

With experience, marketing research analysts eventually are assigned their own research projects. Those considering careers as marketing research analysts should be able to work accurately, because much time is spent on data analysis. Patience and persistence are necessary qualities, since marketing research analysts must spend long hours on independent study and problem solving. At the same time, they must work well with others; marketing research analysts often oversee interviews for a wide variety of individuals.

Marketing research analysts must be able to present their findings, both orally and in writing, in a clear, meaningful way.

Marketing, Sales, and Public Relations Manager

A wide range of educational backgrounds are suitable for entry into marketing, sales, and public relations managerial jobs, but many employers prefer a broad liberal arts background. A bachelor's degree in economics, sociology, psychology, literature, or philosophy, among other subjects, is acceptable. However, requirements vary depending upon the particular job.

For marketing and sales management positions, some employers prefer a bachelor's or master's degree in business administration with an emphasis on marketing. Courses in economics, business law, accounting, finance, mathematics, and statistics are also highly recommended.

In highly technical industries, such as computer and electronics manufacturing, a bachelor's degree in engineering or science combined with a master's degree in business administration may be preferred.

For public relations management positions, some employers prefer a bachelor's or master's degree in public relations or journalism. The individual's curriculum should include courses in advertising, business administration, public affairs, political science, and creative and technical writing. For all these specialties, courses in management and completion of an internship while in school are highly recommended. Familiarity with computerized word-processing and database applications also are important for many marketing and public relations management positions.

Most marketing, sales, and public relations management positions are filled by promoting experienced staff or related professional or technical personnel, such as sales representatives, purchasing agents, buyers, product or brand specialists, advertising specialists, promotion specialists, and public relations specialists.

In small firms, where the number of positions is limited, advancement to a management position may come slowly. In large firms, promotion may occur more quickly.

Although experience, ability, and leadership are emphasized for promotion, advancement may be accelerated by participation in management training programs conducted by many large firms. Many firms also provide their employees with continuing education opportunities, either in-house or at local colleges and universities, and encourage employee participation in seminars and conferences, often provided by professional societies. Often in collaboration with colleges and universities, numerous marketing and related associations sponsor national or local management training programs. Courses include brand and product management, international marketing, sales management evaluation, telemarketing and direct sales, promotion, marketing communication, market research, organizational communication, and data-processing systems procedures and management. Many firms pay all or part of the cost for those who successfully complete courses.

Some associations (listed in Appendix A) offer certification programs for marketing, advertising, and public relations managers. Certification is a sign of competence and achievement that is particularly important in a competitive job market. While relatively few marketing, sales, and public relations managers currently are certified, the number of managers seeking certification is expected to grow. For example, Sales and Marketing Executives International offers a management certification program based on education and job performance. The Public Relations Society of America offers an accreditation program for public relations practitioners based on years of experience and an examination. The American Marketing Association is developing a certification program for marketing managers.

People interested in becoming marketing, sales, and public relations managers should be mature, creative, highly motivated, resistant to stress, and flexible yet decisive. The ability to communicate persuasively, both orally and in writing, with other managers, staff, and the public is vital.

Marketing, sales, and public relations managers also need tact, good judgment, and exceptional ability to establish and maintain effective personal relationships with supervisory and professional staff members and client firms.

Because of the importance and high visibility of their jobs, marketing, sales, and public relations managers often are prime candidates for advancement. Well-trained, experienced, successful managers may be promoted to higher positions in their own or other firms. Some become top executives. Managers with extensive experience and sufficient capital may open their own businesses.

CAREER OUTLOOK

Marketing Research Analyst

Employment of marketing research analysts is expected to grow about as fast as the average for all occupations through 2006. Most job openings, however, are likely to result from the need to replace experienced workers who transfer to other occupations, retire, or leave the labor force for other reasons.

Demand for qualified marketing research analysts should be strong due to an increasingly competitive economy. Marketing research provides organizations with valuable feedback from purchasers, allowing companies to evaluate consumer satisfaction and more effectively plan for the future.

With companies seeking to expand their market and consumers become better informed, the need for marketing professionals is increasing. Opportunities for marketing research analysts with graduate degrees should be good in a wide range of employment settings, particularly in marketing research firms, as companies find it more profitable to contract out for marketing research services rather than support their own marketing department.

Other organizations, including financial services organizations, health care institutions, advertising firms, manufacturing firms producing consumer goods, and insurance companies, may offer job opportunities for marketing research analysts.

A strong background in marketing, mathematics, statistics, and econometrics provides the basis for acquiring any specialty within the field. Those skilled in quantitative techniques and their application to marketing research using computers should have the best job opportunities.

Like economists, marketing research graduates with related work experience in a closely related business field or industry should have the best job opportunities.

Those with only a bachelor's degree but who have a strong background in mathematics, statistics, survey design, and computer science may be hired by private firms as research assistants.

Marketing, Sales, and Public Relations Manager

These jobs are highly coveted and will be sought by other managers or highly experienced professional and technical personnel, resulting in substantial job competition. College graduates with extensive experience, a high level of creativity, and strong communication skills should have the best job opportunities. Those who have new media and interactive marketing skills will be particularly sought after.

Employment of marketing, sales, and public relations managers is expected to increase faster than the average for all occupations through 2006. Increasingly intense domestic and global competition in products and services offered to consumers should require greater marketing, promotional, and public relations efforts by managers. Management and public relations firms may experience particularly rapid growth as businesses increasingly hire contractors for these services rather than support additional full-time staff.

Projected employment growth varies by industry. For example, employment of marketing, sales, and public relations managers is expected to grow faster than average in most business services industries, such as computer and data-processing and management and public relations firms, while average growth is projected in manufacturing industries overall. Many companies that eliminated in-house marketing and advertising departments during downsizing in recent years are now relying on firms that specialize in promotion, marketing, and advertising activities to provide these services.

SAMPLE JOB ADVERTISEMENTS

To get an idea of the kind of positions available, examine the sample job announcements in Exhibits 11.1 and 11.2. (Contact information is not provided here because these particular positions have already been filled.)

Exhibit 11.1

Regional Marketing Analyst Announcement

Job Title: Regional Marketing Analyst

Location: California

Description: This position requires an individual with 8+ years supervisory experience. Product pricing and business planning knowledge a plus. Must understand nature of insurance industry. Strong analytical skills and oral and written communications skills are required. Bachelors in economics, business, finance, or mathematics is a must.

Duties: Make presentations to groups, multitasking, organizing and planning. Very visible position with light travel, will interface with multiple departments in various offices regarding preparation, analysis, presentation of product pricing, and business and strategic planning. Ability to grow into Regional Finance & Administration Manager position.

Exhibit 11.2

Senior Marketing Project Director Announcement

Job Title: Senior Marketing Project Director

Location: Massachusetts

Description: Responsible for (1) managing all facets of complex studies from beginning to completion of product, including scheduling studies, designing questionnaires, designing table specs, and data checking, and (2) monitoring and ensuring project schedules are met within budget.

Position involves overseeing implementation of various consumer surveys, ensuring data accuracy and timely delivery of data to clients. Some statistics course work desirable (one or two classes). High-pressure environment.

Qualifications: Economics, psychology, sociology, or math degree desired. Highly organized. Detail oriented. Basic survey research and/or data collection methods experience required. One to two years of market research experience.

SALARIES

According to a recent salary survey by the National Association of Colleges and Employers, graduates with a bachelor's degree in marketing received offerings averaging $27,900, and those with a bachelor's degree in economics received slightly higher offers, averaging $31,300 a year.

The median annual salary of marketing, sales, and public relations managers was $46,000 in 1996. The lowest 10 percent earned $23,000 or less, while the top 10 percent earned $97,000 or more. Many earned bonuses equal to 10 percent or more of their salaries.

Surveys show that salary levels vary substantially, depending upon the level of managerial responsibility, length of service, education, and employer's size, location, and industry. For example, manufacturing firms generally pay marketing, sales, and public relations managers higher salaries than do non-manufacturing firms. For sales managers, the size of their sales territory is another important determinant of salary.

According to a survey by Abbot, Langer and Associates, of Crete, Illinois, annual incomes for sales/marketing managers varied greatly from under $25,000 to over $250,000, depending on the manager's level of education, experience, industry, and the number of employees he or she supervises.

According to a recent survey by *Advertising Age* magazine, average annual salaries are as follows:

Vice president brand manager	$79,000
Vice president product manager	$105,000
Vice president advertising	$130,000
Vice president marketing	$133,000

According to a recent survey by the Public Relations Society of America, senior public relations managers earned an average of $76,790.

Another survey shows that market research managers had an average salary of $85,000.

CLOSE-UP

CHRIS FULLER, GENERAL MANAGER, MARKETING AND SALES

Chris Fuller has been in marketing and sales for more than thirty years, working his way up through a variety of responsible positions. He was employed by Colgate Palmolive, General Foods, Pepsi Cola, and Thomas J. Lipton and retired in 1988.

He earned his B.A. in economics and his M.B.A., both from Dartmouth College.

Getting Started

"What attracted me to this field was that it was glamorous in a way. You had a lot of advertising and promotion. Product managers made good money, the businesses were stable, and you didn't have the big hiring and firing problems we have in the '90s. You could stay with a company for a long time. They had good programs and they were well respected in the business community all around the United States.

"I got my B.A. in economics and my M.B.A., both at Dartmouth College. That was back in 1953. I've been in this business for thirty years. I started with Colgate Palmolive in 1956. They were in the household products business, which sold products through the same channels as the food companies. They ended up in the same stores.

"At General Foods, I was manager of marketing analysis and then became a product manager in the frozen potato business. At Pepsi Cola I was vice president of finance and president of Metrop Bottling Company, which sold Pepsi through company-owned franchises in the United States.

"I went to work for Thomas J. Lipton in 1977. I was senior vice president of operations and finance there, then became senior vice president of general management. That was a marketing job, where I managed a group of businesses."

What the Work Is Like

"Food service is a secondary business within the framework of a retail business in most food companies—General Foods, or Nabisco, or Procter and Gamble, for example. Food service is usually a much smaller part of their business and normally a less profitable part of the business.

"The purpose of the food service industry, at least at Thomas J. Lipton, was to sell company products, such as tea bags, and try and get them exposed into restaurants and cafeterias—wherever food was sold throughout the United States. The retail end deals with supermarkets and smaller

continued

continued
mom-and-pop stores. Food service is designed to sell products to restaurants.

"There are several functions in a food service business. One is to take the products that a retail business is selling and get them designed in the right sizes and the right types of packages to sell to restaurants. You don't necessarily sell the same product to a restaurant that you would to a consumer through a food store.

"You have to take the entire line of products you want to sell to restaurants and have them redesigned for the restaurant trade. When I was there, the major product happened to be tea bags. A tea bag that you sell to a consumer is for one cup of tea. The tea bag you'd sell to a restaurant might be for a whole jug of tea.

"The taste could be slightly different as well. For example, you may sell a very spicy product, but the restaurant doesn't want a spicy product; their clientele prefers milder tastes. Sometimes you can accommodate them, sometimes you can't, depending on how many other restaurants are in the same boat.

"Another function is marketing. Marketing is pricing, packaging, and the development of the particular product you're going to advertise, promote, and sell. You advertise in the trade journals to let customers know you're going to be offering a particular product.

"Marketing also includes sales. We worked as part of a team. We had a finance person, for example, who would tell us if we were making money or not or what kind of prices we needed in order to profit on something. This position often holds a profit responsibility. If he spends too much money, the business will lose money and he's the guy who will go out the door.

"The sales guys, although responsible for sales volume and reaching a quota every week, do not have any profit responsibility, and they are always asking for lower prices, more advertising, and more promotion. The marketing guy says, 'You can't have that much, because if we spend that much and price the product ten cents a case less, we're going to lose money.' Marketing and sales are often at odds with each other. Budget time, there is always a battle.

"I had many businesses I was responsible for. My particular job encompassed the Good Humor business and some other odds and ends. The ice cream business is enormous and very important within Lipton. They also had a little Mideast business called Sahadi and they sold fruit rolls and other products to restaurants in areas where you had a high concentration of Middle Eastern people.

"Lipton also has a dry soup business, Wishbone salad dressing, and they have noodles and sauce and rice and sauce businesses. Sometimes we could get that sold through restaurants if they didn't want to make that product themselves. Most restaurants like to make their own pasta though, but some don't.

"I had a person I supervised who managed the day to day of the food service end, and his job was to decide what pricing promotions and advertising were needed that month to sell the product. He also decided how many salespeople he needed, what kind of training they should have, where they should be stationed, which accounts those salespeople would call on, and how much time they could give to each account.

"Food service salespeople cover a lot more territory than the retail sales end. The volume is generally lower, so you can't afford to have too many salespeople.

"There's a lot of automobile travel and a very tough schedule. Sometimes the accounts will see you when you want to see them; sometimes you have to wait and see them another day and here you are, having traveled three hundred miles. So, what are you going to do if you don't have it planned to see other accounts in that area? There's a lot of planning and time away from home. It affects family life very negatively.

"The sales manager has to go out and see sales reps because they can't afford to take the time to come to you and lose sales. So, the sales manager is out in the field with personnel too, making calls and making sure the reps are using the right techniques and handling each situation the way it should be handled in order to get the maximum sales volume.

"A step up from that, in marketing, your traveling would be a lot less. The sales manager would normally report to the vice president of marketing. Sales is part of the marketing mix.

continued

continued

"Although marketing is a step up, there's a downside to it. If they're not making the expected profit, they can lose their jobs. They have the same sales volume responsibility that the salespeople have because the salespeople report to them.

"They make an agreement with sales—they say, for example, okay, we're going to sell one hundred units of X to, say, Denny's. Now say they only sell ninety units. The sales guy has the first responsibility, and the marketing person does too. He had agreed that that was what could be sold with the certain advertising, price, and quality of the product. But he missed it, so he's also on the line.

"It's extraordinarily time consuming in this business; it never ends. No marketing job in today's environment is nine to five. There is always competition.

"The upside is that most successful salespeople like their job. You have to like it. If you don't like walking in and talking to people every day, this job isn't for you.

"There's a lot of shmoozing that goes on. You get to know the purchasing person, and if you've been calling on him for a number of years, theoretically, you'd better get to know who his wife is and who the kids are and when their birthdays are and take him out to dinner. You're not giving expensive presents—those are out—but little courtesies are okay.

"Money is no better than it is in retail. I wouldn't say that the money is terrific. It's hard work; you're not going to end up being wealthy. But you get a good pension plan, and you get bonuses.

"To run a sales organization, you have to base it on who does what. There are a lot of incentives: trips, prizes, and cash.

"When you're selling food, you're selling the brand name or a recipe. You're not selling what it can do—you're selling recognition. You might cook up a batch of macaroni and cheese for the purchaser to sample, but it's not the same as selling a computer or a car. You don't have to know how to cook. So you say, 'I don't know how to cook, but the directions here are so simple even I can do this. Just give me a pot and water, and I'll show you. If you're selling a car, you have to know all the things that that car has, the features it has. It's much more complex. Food service is much simpler in some ways."

Advice from Chris Fuller

"The most important thing is that you don't mind traveling and that you like to meet people and talk to people every day. You have to be able to follow directions. You're going to have a regional manager or a division manager over you, and they will be giving you directions and you will have to follow those directions explicitly.

"What you do every day is tracked—where you have been, who you have seen, and what you have sold. Every day. You are in a fishbowl. Every salesperson in the United States has got his working life on a computer somewhere.

"You need to be a gregarious person, and you have to be thick-skinned and able to take criticism. You can get a lot of complaints from a customer. A shipment didn't come in on time. Or he thinks he was shorted or the macaroni and cheese didn't taste the same as the batch you cooked up for him that day. Are you sure it's the same product? All that kind of thing. There's constant haranguing. The purchasing agent you're dealing with has been criticized by his boss and the first guy that's going to walk through that door—you—is going to get it.

"If you go into food service, in order to advance you might want to move over to the retail side at a later date, selling to supermarkets. Your eventual aim is to go up the ladder in sales and then go into marketing. A lot of people from sales go into marketing. You need to start young, when you're in your twenties, and then move over to marketing in your early thirties. If you don't move to marketing in your early thirties, it will be too late and you'll get stuck in sales. There's a corporate system you have to learn and follow.

"But it's a good career. It's a stable business. The companies that are in it are solid. They're not fly-by-night. For the most part, they're not going to go out of business.

"You have to get up and do something every day; you can't rest on your laurels. If you like people and competition, you'll be fine."

CHAPTER TWELVE

PATH 3: HUMAN RESOURCES

*E*conomics majors choosing careers in the field of human resource management are responsible for allocating labor within the firm, establishing appropriate incentive structures for workers, designing and implementing fringe benefits packages, and establishing the process and criteria for hiring and promotion.

Attracting the most qualified employees available and matching them to the jobs for which they are best suited is important for the success of any organization. However, many enterprises are too large to permit close contact between top management and employees. Instead, personnel, training, and labor relations specialists and managers, commonly known as human resources specialists and managers, provide this link. These individuals recruit and interview employees and advise on hiring decisions in accordance with policies and requirements that have been established in conjunction with top management.

In an effort to improve morale and productivity and limit job turnover, they also help their firms effectively use employees' skills, provide training opportunities to enhance those skills, and boost employees' satisfaction with their jobs and working conditions.

Although some jobs in the human resources field require only limited contact with people outside the office, most involve frequent contact. Dealing with people is an essential part of the job. In a small organization, one person may handle all aspects of personnel, training, and labor relations work.

In contrast, in a large corporation the top human resources executive usually develops and coordinates personnel programs and policies. These policies usually are implemented by a director or manager of human resources and, in some cases, a director of industrial relations.

DEFINITION OF THE CAREER PATHS

Within the human resources field, there is a wide range of job titles and responsibilities:

Human Resources Director

The director of human resources may oversee several departments, each headed by an experienced manager, who most likely specializes in one personnel activity, such as employment, compensation, benefits, training and development, or employee relations.

Employment Manager

Employment and placement managers oversee the hiring and separation of employees and supervise various workers, including equal employment opportunity specialists and recruitment specialists.

Recruiter

Recruiters maintain contacts within the community and may travel extensively—often to college campuses—to search for promising job applicants. Recruiters screen, interview, and, in some cases, test applicants. They may also check references and extend offers of employment to qualified candidates. These workers need to be thoroughly familiar with the organization and its personnel policies to discuss wages, working conditions, and promotional opportunities with prospective employees. They also need to remain informed about equal employment opportunity (EEO) and affirmative action guidelines and laws, such as the Americans with Disabilities Act.

EEO/Affirmative Action Coordinator

Large organizations often employ special EEO representatives or affirmative action coordinators. They investigate and resolve EEO grievances, examine corporate practices for possible violations, and compile and submit EEO statistical reports.

Employer Relations Representative

Employer relations representatives, who usually work in government agencies, maintain working relationships with local employers and promote the use of public employment programs and services.

Employment Interviewer

Employment interviewers, sometimes called personnel consultants, help match job seekers with employers.

Job Analyst

Job analysts, sometimes called position classifiers, perform very exacting work. They collect and examine detailed information about job duties to prepare job descriptions. These descriptions explain the duties, training, and skills each job requires. Whenever a large organization introduces a new job or reviews existing jobs, it calls upon the expert knowledge of the job analyst.

Occupational Analyst

Occupational analysts conduct research, generally in large firms. They are concerned with occupational classification systems and study the effects of industry and occupational trends upon worker relationships. They may serve as technical liaison between the firm and industry, government, and labor unions.

Compensation Manager

Establishing and maintaining a firm's pay system is the principal job of the compensation manager. Assisted by staff specialists, compensation managers devise ways to ensure fair and equitable pay rates. They may conduct surveys to see how their rates compare with others and to see that the firm's pay scale complies with changing laws and regulations.

In addition, compensation managers often oversee their firm's performance evaluation system, and they may design reward systems such as pay-for-performance plans.

Employee Benefits Manager

Employee benefits managers handle the company's employee benefits program, notably its health insurance and pension plans. Expertise in designing and administering benefits programs continues to gain importance as employer-provided benefits account for a growing proportion of overall compensation costs, and as benefit plans increase in number and complexity. For example, pension benefits might include savings and thrift, profit sharing,

and stock ownership plans; health benefits may include long-term cata-
strophic illness insurance and dental insurance. Familiarity with health benefits is a top priority at present, as more firms struggle to cope with the rising
cost of health care for employees and retirees.

In addition to health insurance and pension coverage, some firms offer
their employees life and accidental death and dismemberment insurance, disability insurance, and relatively new benefits designed to meet the needs of
a changing workforce, such as parental leave, child care and elder care, long-
term nursing home care insurance, employee assistance and wellness programs,
and flexible benefits plans. Benefits managers must keep abreast of changing
federal and state regulations and legislation that may affect employee benefits.

Employee Assistance Plan Manager

Employee assistance plan managers, also called employee welfare managers,
are responsible for a wide array of programs covering occupational safety and
health standards and practices; health promotion and physical fitness, medical examinations and minor health treatment, such as first aid; plant security; publications; food service and recreation activities; car pooling; employee
suggestion systems; child care and elder care; and counseling services. Child
and elder care are increasingly important due to growth in the number of
dual-income households and the elderly population. Counseling may help
employees deal with emotional disorders, alcoholism, or marital, family, consumer, legal, and financial problems. Career counseling and second career
counseling for employees approaching retirement age also may be provided.
In large firms, some of these programs, such as security and safety, are in
separate departments headed by other managers.

Training and Development Managers

Training is supervised by training and development managers. Increasingly,
management recognizes that training offers a way of developing skills,
enhancing productivity and quality of work, and building loyalty to the firm.
Training is widely accepted as a method of improving employee morale, but
this is only one of the reasons for its growing importance. Other factors
include the complexity of the work environment, the rapid pace of organizational and technological change, and the growing number of jobs in fields
that constantly generate new knowledge. In addition, advances in learning
theory have provided insights into how adults learn and how training can be
organized most effectively for them.

Training specialists plan, organize, and direct a wide range of training activities. Trainers conduct orientation sessions and arrange on-the-job training
for new employees. They help rank-and-file workers maintain and improve

their job skills and possibly prepare for jobs requiring greater skill. They help supervisors improve their interpersonal skills in order to deal effectively with employees. They may set up individualized training plans to strengthen an employee's existing skills or to teach new ones.

Training specialists in some companies set up programs to develop executive potential among employees in lower-level positions.

In government-supported training programs, training specialists function as case managers. They first assess the training needs of clients, and then guide them through the most appropriate training method. After training, clients may either be referred to employer relations representatives or receive job placement assistance.

Planning and program development is an important part of the training specialist's job. In order to identify and assess training needs within the firm, trainers may confer with managers and supervisors or conduct surveys. They also periodically evaluate training effectiveness.

Depending on the size, goals, and nature of the organization, trainers may differ considerably in their responsibilities and in the methods they use. Training methods include on-the-job training; schools in which shop conditions are duplicated for trainees prior to putting them on the shop floor; apprenticeship training; classroom training; programmed instruction, which may involve interactive videos, videodiscs, and other computer-aided instructional technologies; simulators; conferences; and workshops.

International Human Resources Manager

An emerging specialist title is that of international human resources manager, who handles human resources issues related to a company's foreign operations.

Human Resources Information System Specialist

Human resources information system specialist is another emerging position. This specialist develops and applies computer programs to process personnel information, match job seekers with job openings, and handle other personnel matters.

ADDITIONAL PATHS

Although often considered a separate field, labor and industrial relations can also sometimes fall into the realm of human resources and is a viable career path for economics majors.

Industrial Relations Director

The director of industrial relations forms labor policy, oversees industrial labor relations, negotiates collective bargaining agreements, and coordinates grievance procedures to handle complaints resulting from disputes under the contract for firms with unionized employees. The director of industrial relations also advises and collaborates with the director of human resources and other managers and members of their staff, because all aspects of personnel policy, such as wages, benefits, pensions, and work practices, may be involved in drawing up a new or revised contract.

Labor Relations Manager

Industrial labor relations programs are implemented by labor relations managers and their staff. When a collective bargaining agreement is up for negotiation, labor relations specialists prepare information for management to use during negotiation, which requires familiarity with economic and wage data, as well as extensive knowledge of labor law and collective bargaining trends. The labor relations staff interprets and administers the contract with respect to grievances, wages and salaries, employee welfare, health care, pensions, union and management practices, and other contractual stipulations. As union membership is continuing to decline in most industries, industrial relations personnel are working more with employees who are not members of a labor union.

Dispute Resolution Specialist

Dispute resolution—that is, attaining tacit or contractual agreements—has become increasingly important as parties to a dispute attempt to avoid costly litigation, strikes, or other disruptions. Dispute resolution also has become more complex, involving employees, management, unions, other firms, and government agencies. Specialists involved in dispute resolution must be highly knowledgeable and experienced, and they often report to the director of industrial relations.

A conciliator, or mediator, advises and counsels labor and management to prevent and, when necessary, resolve disputes over labor agreements or other labor relations issues.

An arbitrator, sometimes called an umpire or referee, decides disputes that bind both labor and management to specific terms and conditions of labor contracts.

Labor relations specialists who work for unions perform many of the same functions on behalf of the union and its members.

THE QUALIFICATIONS YOU'LL NEED

Because of the diversity of duties and level of responsibility, the educational backgrounds of human resources, personnel, training, and labor relations specialists and managers vary considerably.

In filling entry-level jobs, firms generally seek college graduates. Some employers prefer applicants who have majored in economics, human resources, personnel administration, or industrial and labor relations, while others look for college graduates with a technical or business background. Still others feel that a well-rounded liberal arts education is best.

Because an interdisciplinary background is appropriate for work in this area, a combination of courses in the social sciences, business, and behavioral sciences is useful. Some jobs may require a background in engineering, science, finance, or law. Most prospective personnel specialists should take courses in compensation, recruitment, training and development, and performance appraisal, as well as courses in principles of management, organizational structure, and industrial psychology. Other relevant courses include business administration, public administration, psychology, sociology, political science, economics, and statistics.

Courses in labor law, collective bargaining, labor economics, labor history, and industrial psychology also provide a valuable background for the prospective labor relations specialist. Knowledge of computers and information systems is important for some jobs.

Graduate study in industrial or labor relations is increasingly important for those seeking work in labor relations. A law degree seldom is required for entry-level jobs, but many people responsible for contract negotiations are lawyers, and a combination of industrial relations courses and law is highly desirable. A background in law is also desirable for employee benefits managers and others who must interpret the growing number of laws and regulations.

A degree in dispute resolution provides an excellent background for mediators, arbitrators, and related personnel. A master's degree in personnel, training, or labor relations, or in a specialty of economics, or in business administration with a concentration in human resources management is desirable for those seeking general and top management positions.

For many specialized jobs in this field, previous experience is an asset; for managerial positions, it is essential. Many employers prefer entry-level workers who have gained some experience through an internship or work-study program while in school. Personnel administration and human resources development require the ability to work with individuals, as well as a commitment to organizational goals. This field also demands other skills that people may develop elsewhere—computer usage, spreadsheet and database familiarity, selling, teaching, supervising, and volunteering, among others.

Personnel, training, and labor relations specialists and managers should speak and write effectively and be able to work with and/or supervise people of all levels of education and experience as part of a team. They must be patient to cope with conflicting points of view and emotionally stable to deal with the unexpected and the unusual. The ability to function under pressure is essential. Integrity, fair-mindedness, and a persuasive, congenial personality are important qualities.

Recent economics graduates can start as entry-level workers, often participating in formal or on-the-job training programs in which they learn how to classify jobs, interview applicants, or administer employee benefits. Next, they are assigned to specific areas in the personnel department to gain experience. Later, they may advance to a managerial position, overseeing a major element of the personnel program—compensation or training, for example.

Exceptional personnel, training, and labor relations workers may be promoted to director of personnel or industrial relations, which can eventually lead to a top managerial or executive position. Others may join a consulting firm or open their own business.

Though not widespread, some organizations offer certification examinations to members who meet certain education and experience requirements. Certification is a sign of competence and can enhance one's advancement opportunities. (Several of these organizations are listed in Appendix A.)

JOB SETTINGS

Personnel, training, and labor relations specialists and managers hold more than 513,000 jobs nationwide. They are employed in virtually every industry. Specialists account for three out of five positions; managers, two out of five. About 9,000—mostly specialists—are self-employed, working as consultants to public and private employers.

The private sector accounts for about 85 percent of salaried jobs. Among these salaried jobs, services industries—including business, health, social, management, and educational services—account for four out of ten jobs; labor organizations—the largest employer among specific industries—account for one out of ten.

Manufacturing industries account for two out of ten jobs, while finance, insurance, and real estate firms account for about one out of ten.

SAMPLE JOB ADVERTISEMENTS

To get an idea of the kind of positions available, examine the sample job announcements in Exhibits 12.1 through 12.6. (Contact information is not provided here because these particular positions have already been filled.)

Exhibit 12.1

Consultant Announcement

Job Title: Consultant/senior consultant

Location: New York, New York

Description: Opening with a management consulting firm that provides services to clients in the telecommunications, entertainment, and cable industries. Leadership potential exists for the right individuals within the telecom operations group of the New York practice, which focuses on OSS strategies and IP related offerings.

Qualifications: Ideal candidates will possess a minimum of two to eight years' industry experience with strong quantitative and analytical skills, including statistics. An understanding of economics, engineering, accounting, and finance and an appreciation for information technology are essential. A willingness to travel 50 percent of the time is also required.

Exhibit 12.2

Business Development Manager Announcement

Job Title: Business development manager

Location: California

Description: With minimal supervision, this person will conduct research into prospective external business partnerships, negotiate terms, obtain internal approvals, and drive them to closure. The applicant must interface with multiple job functions, which include finance, legal, sales, product management, and senior management. Additionally, the applicant must be able to manage external partners and proper execution of contracts.

Qualifications: General knowledge of PCs, Windows, Windows 95/98, and NT is a must. M.B.A. preferred, or postgraduate course work that includes business law, contracts, economics, corporate accounting, and marketing. B.S. in economics/business/political science or equivalent work experience.

Exhibit 12.3

U.S. Compensation Manager Announcement

Job Title: U.S. compensation manager

Location: Texas

Description: As a member of the Human Resources U.S. Compensation team, you will assume a lead role in ensuring all components of compensation are competitive in the United States. The ideal candidate will be an expert in the effective development, implementation, and utilization of creative compensation tools. This position provides a dotted-line leadership/guidance to all U.S. site compensation staff. You will be responsible for defining appropriate skill-level requirements for all U.S. sites and identifying appropriate development activities to bridge gaps. Effectively involves sites in developing and evaluating U.S. programs. Ensures sites are properly using tools developed. Represents U.S. perspective in evaluating global compensation tools.

Qualifications: The ideal candidate will have two years of recent compensation experience, as well as leadership and influence skills and a professional demeanor. Must derive great pleasure from accuracy. Ability to identify meaningful analysis. Represent strong point of view that is backed with solid factual data. B.A./B.S.—economics, business, human resources, mathematics, or related field.

Exhibit 12.4

Business Analyst Announcement

Job Title: Health care/managed care business analyst

continued

continued

Location: Washington, D.C.

Description: Dedicate your talents to producing analyses for strategic decisions on companies, industries, and emerging business topics including analyses of trends, competitive landscape, macroeconomics, and key industry drivers and processes.

Qualifications: Requires a bachelor's degree (master's preferred), with three or more years' experience in business analysis or industry research, management consulting, or business strategic planning in the health care/managed care industry. Beyond your superior team working, multitasking, and deadline and interpersonal/ communication skills, you must have proven business analysis and writing abilities and be familiar with all necessary research tools. Proficiency in MS Office and Lotus Notes is preferred. French/English bilingual is a plus.

Exhibit 12.5

Health Care Analyst Announcement

Job Title: Health care analyst

Location: Kansas City, Missouri

Description: We provide comprehensive medical services for more than 1.5 million military family members. We have opportunities at various levels for health care analysts to assess cost, utilization, and enrollment data to develop reports.

Qualifications: Requires a bachelor's degree in economics, health care, statistics, mathematics, or business. Proficiency with computer programming and Excel required. Prefer SAS programming skills. A working knowledge of the health care industry, especially HMOs, is a plus.

Exhibit 12.6

Contracts Administration Announcement

Job Title: Contracts administrator

Location: Madison, Wisconsin

Description: Large corporation in Madison suburb has an immediate opening for a contracts administrator. This position will work with the company's domestic clientele. Duties include preparing contract modifications and amendments, tracking contract milestones, maintaining contract pricing, and preparing sales history reports. This company offers room for career advancement. Excellent benefits package.

Qualifications: Two or three years of contracts experience and/or a four-year degree in economics, business, or a related field.

CAREER OUTLOOK

The number of personnel, training, and labor relations specialists and managers is expected to grow faster than the average for all occupations through 2005. As in other occupations, job growth among specialists is projected to outpace job growth among managers. In addition, many job openings will result from the need to replace workers who leave this occupation to transfer to other jobs, retire, or leave for other reasons. However, the job market is likely to remain competitive in view of the abundant supply of qualified college graduates and experienced workers.

Most new jobs for personnel, training, and labor relations specialists and managers will be in the private sector as employers, increasingly concerned about productivity and quality of work, devote greater resources to job-specific training programs in response to the growing complexity of many jobs, the aging of the workforce, and technological advances that can leave employees with obsolete skills.

In addition, legislation and court rulings setting standards in occupational safety and health, equal employment opportunity, wages, and benefits such as health, pension, and family leave will increase demand for experts in these areas. Rising health care costs, in particular, should spur demand for specialists to develop creative compensation and benefits packages that firms can offer prospective employees.

Employment of labor relations staff, including arbitrators and mediators, should grow as firms become more involved in labor relations and attempt to resolve potentially costly labor-management disputes out of court. Increasing demand for international human resources managers and human resources information systems specialists may spur additional job growth.

Employment demand should be strong in management and consulting firms and personnel supply firms as businesses increasingly contract out personnel functions or hire personnel specialists on a contractual basis to meet the increasing cost and complexity of training and development programs. Demand should also increase in firms that develop and administer the increasingly complex employee benefits and compensation packages for other organizations.

Demand for personnel, training, and labor relations specialists and managers also is governed by the staffing needs of the firms where they work. A rapidly expanding business is likely to hire additional personnel workers, either as permanent employees or consultants, while a business that has experienced a merger or a reduction in its workforce will require fewer personnel workers. Also, as human resources management becomes increasingly important to the success of an organization, some small and medium-size businesses that do not have a human resources department may employ workers to perform human resources duties on a part-time basis while maintaining other unrelated responsibilities within the company. In any particular firm, the size and the job duties of the human resources staff are determined by a variety of factors, including the firm's organizational philosophy and goals, the labor intensity and skill profile of the industry, the pace of technological change, government regulations, collective bargaining agreements, standards of professional practice, and labor market conditions.

Factors that could limit job growth include the widespread use of computerized human resources information systems that make workers more productive. As is the case with other workers, employment of personnel, training, and labor relations specialists and managers, particularly in larger firms, may be adversely affected by corporate downsizing and restructuring.

SALARIES

According to a salary survey conducted by the National Association of Colleges and Employers, bachelor's degree candidates entering into human resources fields, including labor relations, received starting offers averaging $25,300 a year in 1996; master's degree candidates received $39,900.

According to a 1996 survey of compensation in the human resources field conducted by Abbott, Langer, and Associates of Crete, Illinois, the median total cash compensation for selected personnel and labor relations occupations was as follows:

Industrial/labor relations directors	$106,100
Divisional human resources directors	$91,300
Compensation and benefits directors	$90,500
Employee/community relations directors	$87,500
Training and organizational directors	$86,600
Benefits directors	$80,500
Plant/location human resources managers	$64,400
Recruitment and interviewing managers	$63,800
Compensation supervisors	$53,400
Training generalists	$49,900
Employment interviewing supervisors	$42,800
Safety specialists	$42,500
Job evaluation specialists	$39,600
Employee assistance/employee counseling specialists	$39,000
Human resources information systems specialists	$38,800
Benefits specialists	$38,300
EEO/affirmative action specialists	$38,200
Training material development specialists	$37,200
Employee services/employee recreation specialists	$35,000

According to a recent survey of workplaces in 160 metropolitan areas, personnel specialists with limited experience had median earnings of $25,700—the middle half earned between $23,700 and $28,500 a year.

Personnel supervisors/managers with limited experience had median earnings of $59,000 a year. The middle half earned between $54,000 and $65,200 a year.

In the federal government in 1997, people with a bachelor's degree or three years' general experience in this field generally started at $19,500 a year. Those with a superior academic record or an additional year of specialized experience started at $24,200 a year. Those with a master's degree may start at $29,600, and those with a doctorate in a personnel field may start at

$35,800. Beginning salaries were slightly higher in areas where the prevailing local pay level was higher. There are no formal entry-level requirements for managerial positions. Applicants must possess a suitable combination of educational attainment, experience, and record of accomplishment.

Personnel specialists in the federal government averaged $52,900 a year in 1997; personnel managers averaged $55,400.

CLOSE-UP

ROBYN BRAMHALL, SENIOR RECRUITER

Robyn Bramhall has been with the human resources department at Fair, Isaac & Company in San Rafael, California, since 1990.

Getting Started

"I had been in a sales department at a large bank and wanted work that brought me closer to people's lives.

"A friend suggested I look at technical recruiting, since I knew a little about technology from my bank job. I had spent five years placing computer professionals on contract assignments.

"Another recruiter told me about this opening, which he had seen advertised in the local paper. I wanted to work closer to home and in a corporate environment as opposed to an agency, so this seemed ideal. I still get to sell, but now it is selling a job and a company to a candidate—and then selling the candidate to the manager."

What the Work Is Like

"I locate, qualify, and present candidates for certain types of positions. Doing this includes lots of phoning, record keeping, E-mailing, database searching, networking, advertising, and meetings.

"There is no typical day for me. Some days I do lots of paperwork, such as when I've just filled a position or need to start a visa process. Other days I spend at a job fair talking to dozens of people about our work.

"I'm always busy, but I usually have many choices of what to do next; if I'm tired of one activity, I can break it up with something else. I talk to such a variety of people each day, and each has a new story to tell.

"Knowing that there's always something else I could be doing to get good people hired, I have to accept that each day must end with the job unfinished. But there are so many small successes each day, I have no problem leaving after a good eight-hour day. When I stay later, it's because I'm engrossed in a project or talking to a candidate—not because it's required. Our company comp-time policy makes me feel better about working more hours, too. I know I'll get to take a breather when I need it.

"What I like the most about my work is learning from all the people I meet and work with. And I learn many things, not just about their work, but also about myself and how I operate in a variety of situations. My coworkers in HR, the managers I'm working for, the people interviewing the candidates, the many people supporting our work internally, and, of course, the candidates, all teach me things about myself and the world.

"The icing on the cake is that I get to look around the company and see the results of my work—lots of new people helping the company grow and succeed.

"Salaries vary greatly in recruiting. I was on a base plus commission plan at the agency, and I am now on base plus company bonus plus personal bonus plan. I made more at the agency I worked at before, but I wasn't happy and the benefits were not as robust. As a staff recruiter, you will not get rich, but you can make a comfortable living."

Advice from Robyn Bramhall

"Since I came into this field through the back door, I can't say that anyone should follow my footsteps. The good news is that it doesn't take any special training to be a good recruiter; but it doesn't hurt to know something about a certain industry or type of work, especially if it involves technology. A good sense of equity, privacy, integrity, empathy, and humor also helps."

CHAPTER THIRTEEN

PATH 4: BANKING, FINANCE, AND INVESTMENT

A natural path for economics majors is a career in banking, finance, or investment. Within each sector, duties and responsibilities vary considerably but each allows the economics major the chance to utilize the analytical skills he or she has amassed during college.

DEFINITION OF THE CAREER PATHS

Banking

Although banks and other financial institutions generally fill higher-level positions from within, they do make management trainee programs available to college graduates. Economics majors tend to be particularly well prepared for these positions. These management trainee positions generally require individuals to spend some time working as a bank teller. But after gaining some seniority and showing aptitude, tellers with a degree in economics can go on to become bank managers and loan officers.

Financial institutions such as banks, savings and loan associations, credit unions, personal credit institutions, and finance companies may serve as depositories for cash and financial instruments and offer loans, investment counseling, consumer credit, trust management, and other financial services.

Some specialize in specific financial services. Financial managers in financial institutions include vice presidents, who may head one or more departments, bank branch managers, savings and loan association managers, consumer credit managers, and credit union managers. These managers make decisions in accordance with policy set by the institution's board of directors and federal and state laws and regulations.

Because of changing regulations and increased government scrutiny, financial managers in financial institutions must place greater emphasis on accurate reporting of financial data. They must have detailed knowledge of industries allied to banking, such as insurance, real estate, and securities, and a broad knowledge of business and industrial activities. With growing domestic and foreign competition, knowledge of an expanding and increasingly complex variety of financial services is becoming a necessity for financial managers in financial institutions and other corporations.

Besides supervising financial services, financial managers in financial institutions may advise individuals and businesses on financial planning.

Loan Officer and Loan Counselor. Banks and other financial institutions need up-to-date information on companies and individuals applying for loans and credit. Customers and clients provide this information to the financial institution's loan officers and counselors, generally the first employees they will see.

Loan officers prepare, analyze, and verify loan applications, make decisions regarding the extension of credit, and help borrowers fill out loan applications.

Loan counselors help consumers with low income or a poor credit history qualify for credit, usually a home mortgage.

Loan officers usually specialize in commercial, consumer, or mortgage loans. Commercial or business loans help companies pay for new equipment or expand operations. Consumer loans include home equity, automobile, and personal loans. Mortgage loans are made to purchase real estate or to refinance an existing mortgage.

Loan officers represent lending institutions that provide funds for a variety of purposes. Personal loans can be made to consolidate bills, purchase expensive items, such as an automobile or furniture, or finance a college education.

Loan officers attempt to lower their firm's risk by receiving collateral—security pledged for the payment of a loan. For example, when lending money for a college education, the bank may insist that the borrower offer his or her home as collateral. If the borrower were ever unable to repay the loan, the borrower would have to sell the home to raise the necessary money. Loans backed by collateral also are beneficial to the customer because they generally carry a lower interest rate.

Loan officers and counselors must keep abreast of new financial products and services so they can meet their customers' needs; for example, banks and other lenders now offer a variety of mortgage products, including reverse equity mortgages, shared equity mortgages, and adjustable rate mortgages.

Loan officers meet with customers and gather basic information about the loan request. Often customers will not fully understand the information requested and will call the loan officer for assistance. Once the customer completes the financial forms, the loan officer begins to process them. The loan officer reviews the completed financial forms for accuracy and thoroughness and requests additional information if necessary. For example, the loan officer verifies that the customer has correctly identified the type and purpose of the loan. The loan officer then requests a credit report from one or more of the major credit reporting agencies. This information, along with comments from the loan officer, is included in a loan file and is compared to the lending institution's requirements. Banks and other lenders have established requirements for the maximum percentage of income that can safely go to repay loans. At this point, the loan officer, in consultation with his or her manager, decides whether or not to grant the loan. A loan that would otherwise be denied may be approved if the customer can provide the lender appropriate collateral. Whether or not the loan request is approved, the loan officer informs the borrower of the decision.

Loan counselors meet with consumers who are attempting to purchase a home or refinance debt, but who do not qualify for loans with banks. Often clients rely on income from self-employment or government assistance to prove that they can repay the loan. Counselors also help to psychologically prepare consumers to be homeowners and to pay their debts. Counselors frequently work with clients who have little or no experience with financial matters.

Loan counselors provide positive reinforcement along with the financial tools needed to qualify for a loan. This assistance may take several forms. Occasionally, counselors simply need to explain what information loan officers need to complete a loan transaction. Most of the time loan counselors help clients qualify for a bank-financed mortgage loan. The loan counselor helps the client complete an application and researches federal, state, and local government programs that could provide the money needed for the client to purchase the home. Often, several government programs are combined to provide the necessary money.

Loan officers and counselors usually work in offices, but mortgage loan officers frequently move from office to office and often visit homes of clients while completing a loan request. Commercial loan officers employed by large firms may travel frequently to prepare complex loan agreements.

Most loan officers and counselors work a standard forty-hour week but may work longer, particularly mortgage loan officers who are free to take on as many customers as they choose. Loan officers and counselors usually carry a heavy caseload and sometimes cannot accept new clients until they complete current cases. They are especially busy when interest rates are low, resulting in a surge in loan applications.

Finance

Practically every firm—whether in manufacturing, communications, finance, education, or health care—has one or more financial managers. They may be treasurers, controllers, credit managers, or cash managers; they prepare the financial reports required by the firm to conduct its operations and to ensure that the firm satisfies tax and regulatory requirements. Financial managers also oversee the flow of cash and financial instruments, monitor the extension of credit, assess the risk of transactions, raise capital, analyze investments, develop information to assess the present and future financial status of the firm, and communicate with stockholders and other investors.

In small firms, chief financial officers usually handle all financial management functions. However, in large firms these officers oversee financial management departments and help top managers develop financial and economic policy and establish procedures, delegate authority, and oversee the implementation of these policies.

Highly trained and experienced financial managers head each financial department. Controllers direct the preparation of all financial reports—income statements, balance sheets, and special reports, such as depreciation schedules. They oversee the accounting, audit, or budget departments.

Cash and credit managers monitor and control the flow of cash receipts and disbursements to meet the business and investment needs of the firm. For example, cash flow projections are needed to determine whether loans must be obtained to meet cash requirements, or whether surplus cash may be invested in interest-bearing instruments.

Risk and insurance managers oversee programs to minimize risks and losses that may arise from financial transactions and business operations undertaken by the institution. Credit operations managers establish credit rating criteria, determine credit ceilings, and monitor their institution's extension of credit.

Reserve officers review their institution's financial statements and direct the purchase and sale of bonds and other securities to maintain the asset-liability ratio required by law.

User representatives in international accounting develop integrated international financial and accounting systems for the banking transactions of multinational organizations. A working knowledge of the financial systems of foreign countries is essential.

Investment

Brokers and Investors. Typically, individuals in positions within brokerage and investment firms provide investment advice to individuals and businesses.

Stockbrokers or traders are also called securities sales representatives, registered representatives, or account executives. And it's to these professionals most investors, whether they are individuals with a few hundred dollars to invest or large institutions with millions, turn when buying or selling stocks, bonds, shares in mutual funds, insurance annuities, or other financial products.

When an investor wishes to buy or sell securities, sales representatives may relay the order through their firms' offices to the floor of a securities exchange, such as the New York Stock Exchange. There, securities sales representatives known as brokers' floor representatives buy and sell securities. If a security is not traded on an exchange, the sales representative sends the order to the firm's trading department, where a security trader trades it directly with a dealer in an over-the-counter market, such as the NASDAQ computerized trading system. After the transaction has been completed, the sales representative notifies the customer of the final price.

Securities sales representatives also provide many related services for their customers. Depending on a customer's knowledge of the market, they may explain the meaning of stock market terms and trading practices; offer financial counseling; devise an individual financial portfolio for the client, including securities, life insurance, corporate and municipal bonds, mutual funds, certificates of deposit, annuities, and other investments; and offer advice on the purchase or sale of particular securities.

Not all customers have the same investment goals. Some individuals may prefer long-term investments designed either for capital growth or to provide income over the years; others might want to invest in speculative securities that they hope will rise in price quickly. Securities sales representatives furnish information about the advantages and disadvantages of an investment based on each person's objectives. They also supply the latest price quotations on any security in which the investor is interested, as well as information on the activities and financial positions of the corporations issuing these securities.

Most securities sales representatives serve individual investors, but others specialize in institutional investors. In institutional investing, most sales representatives concentrate on a specific financial product, such as stocks, bonds, options, annuities, or commodity futures. Some handle the sale of new issues, such as corporate securities issued to finance plant expansion.

The most important part of a sales representative's job is finding clients and building a customer base. Thus, beginning securities sales representatives spend much of their time searching for customers, relying heavily on telephone solicitation. They may meet some clients through business and social contacts. Many sales representatives find it useful to get additional exposure by teaching adult education investment courses or by giving lectures at libraries or social clubs. Brokerage firms may give sales representatives lists of people with whom the firm has done business in the past. Sometimes sales representatives may inherit the clients of representatives who have retired.

Financial services sales representatives sell banking and related services. They contact potential customers to explain their services and to ascertain the customer's banking and other financial needs. They may discuss services such as deposit accounts, lines of credit, sales or inventory financing, certificates of deposit, cash management, or investment services. They may solicit businesses to participate in consumer credit card programs.

At most small and medium-size banks, branch managers and commercial loan officers are responsible for marketing the bank's financial services. As banks offer more and increasingly complex financial services—for example, securities brokerage and financial planning—the job of the financial services sales representative is assuming greater importance.

Financial planners develop and implement financial plans for individuals and businesses using their knowledge of tax and investment strategies, securities, insurance, pension plans, and real estate. They interview clients to determine their assets, liabilities, cash flow, insurance coverage, tax status, and financial objectives. Then they analyze all this information and develop a financial plan tailored to each client's needs.

Securities sales representatives usually work in offices where there is much activity. They have access to "quote boards" or computer terminals that continually provide information on the prices of securities.

When sales activity increases, due perhaps to unanticipated changes in the economy, the pace may become very hectic. Established securities sales representatives usually work the same hours as others in the business community. Beginners who are seeking customers may work much longer hours, however. Most securities sales representatives accommodate customers by meeting with them in the evenings or on weekends.

Financial services sales representatives normally work in a comfortable, less stressful office environment. They generally work forty hours a week. They may spend considerable time outside the office meeting with present and prospective clients, attending civic functions, and participating in trade association meetings. Some financial services sales representatives work exclusively inside banks, providing service to "walk-in" customers.

Brokerage Clerk. Brokerage clerks work behind the scenes to produce records associated with financial transactions. Brokerage clerks, who work in the operations areas of securities firms, perform many duties to facilitate the sale and purchase of stocks, bonds, commodities, and other kinds of invest-ments. These clerks produce the necessary records of all transactions that occur in their area of the business.

Job titles depend upon the type of work performed. Purchase-and-sale clerks match orders to buy with orders to sell. They balance and verify stock trades by comparing the records of the selling firm to those of the buying firm. Dividend clerks ensure timely payments of stock or cash dividends to clients of a particular brokerage firm. Transfer clerks execute customer requests for changes to security registration and examine stock certificates for adherence to banking regulations. Receive-and-deliver clerks facilitate the receipt and delivery of securities among firms and institutions. Margin clerks post accounts and monitor activity in customers' accounts. Their job is to ensure that customers make their payments and stay within legal boundaries concerning stock purchases.

A significant and growing number of brokerage clerks use custom-designed software programs to process transactions, allowing transactions to be processed faster than if they were done manually. Currently, only a few cus-tomized accounts are handled manually.

THE QUALIFICATIONS YOU'LL NEED

Training for Bank Tellers and Clerks

When hiring tellers and clerks, banks seek applicants who enjoy public con-tact and have good numerical, clerical, and communication skills. Tellers must feel comfortable handling large amounts of cash and working with comput-ers and video terminals, because their work is highly automated. In some met-ropolitan areas, employers seek multilingual tellers.

Although tellers and clerks work independently, their record keeping is closely supervised. Accuracy and attention to detail are vital.

Tellers should be courteous, attentive, and patient in dealing with the pub-lic, because customers often judge a bank by the way they are treated at the teller window. Maturity, tact, and the ability to quickly explain bank proce-dures and services are important in helping customers complete transactions or make financial decisions.

Many entrants transfer from other occupations; virtually all have at least a high school education. In general, banks prefer applicants who have had high school courses in mathematics, accounting, bookkeeping, economics, and public speaking.

New tellers and clerks at larger banks receive at least one week of formal classroom training. Formal training is followed by several weeks of on-the-job training, during which tellers observe experienced workers before doing the work themselves.

Smaller banks rely primarily upon on-the-job training. In addition to instruction in basic duties, many banks now include extensive training in the bank's products and services—so that tellers can refer customers to appropriate products—communication and sales skills, and instruction on equipment such as ATMs and on-line video terminals.

In large banks, beginners usually start as limited-transaction tellers, cashing checks and processing simple transactions for a few days, before becoming full-service tellers. Often banks simultaneously train tellers for other clerical duties.

Advancement opportunities are good for well-trained, motivated employees. Experienced tellers may advance to head teller, customer service representative, or new accounts clerk. Outstanding tellers who have a college degree or specialized training offered by the banking industry may be promoted to a managerial position.

Banks encourage this upward mobility by providing access to education and other sources of additional training. College graduates with degrees in economics, finance, business, or related fields may participate in management trainee programs, as mentioned earlier in the chapter.

Tellers can prepare for better jobs by taking courses offered or accredited by the American Institute of Banking, an educational affiliate of the American Bankers Association, or the Institute of Financial Education. These organizations have several hundred chapters in cities across the country and numerous study groups in small communities, and they offer correspondence courses. They also work closely with local colleges and universities in preparing courses of study. Most banks use the facilities of these organizations, which assist local banks in conducting cooperative training programs or developing independent training programs.

In addition, many banks refund college tuition fees to their employees upon successful completion of their courses. Although most courses are meant for employed tellers, some community colleges offer preemployment training programs. These programs can help prepare applicants for a job in banking and can give them an advantage over other job seekers.

Training for Finance Careers

A bachelor's degree in economics, accounting, or finance, or in business administration with an emphasis on accounting or finance, is the minimum academic preparation for financial managers. However, a master of business administration (M.B.A.) degree increasingly is valued by employers. Many financial management positions are filled by promoting experienced, technically skilled professional personnel—for example, accountants, budget analysts, credit analysts, insurance analysts, loan officers, and securities analysts—or accounting or related department supervisors in large institutions.

Because of the growing complexity of global trade, shifting federal and state laws and regulations, and a proliferation of new, complex financial instruments, continuing education is becoming vital for financial managers. Firms often provide opportunities for workers to broaden their knowledge and skills and encourage employees to take graduate courses at colleges and universities or attend conferences sponsored by the company.

In addition, financial management, banking, and credit union associations, often in cooperation with colleges and universities, sponsor numerous national or local training programs. People enrolled prepare extensively at home, and then attend sessions on subjects such as accounting management, budget management, corporate cash management, financial analysis, international banking, and data-processing and management information systems. Many firms pay all or part of the costs for those who successfully complete courses. Although experience, ability, and leadership are emphasized for promotion, advancement may be accelerated by this type of special study.

In some cases, financial managers may also broaden their skills and exhibit their competency in specialized fields by attaining professional certification. For example, the Association for Investment Management and Research confers the Chartered Financial Analyst designation to investment professionals who have a bachelor's degree, pass three test levels, and have three or more years of experience in the field. The National Association of Credit Management administers a three-part certification program for business credit professionals.

Through a combination of experience and examinations, these financial managers pass through the level of Credit Business Associate to Credit Business Fellow to Certified Credit Executive.

The Treasury Management Association confers the Certified Cash Manager designation to those who pass an examination and have two years of relevant experience.

Individuals interested in becoming financial managers should enjoy working independently, dealing with people, and analyzing detailed account information. The ability to communicate effectively, both orally and in writing, is also important. They also need tact, good judgment, and the ability to establish effective personal relationships to oversee staff.

Financial analysis and management have been revolutionized by technological improvements in personal computers and data-processing equipment. Knowledge of their applications is vital to upgrade managerial skills and to enhance advancement opportunities.

Because financial management is critical for efficient business operations, well-trained, experienced financial managers who display a strong grasp of the operations of various departments within their organization are prime candidates for promotion to top management positions.

Some financial managers transfer to closely related positions in other industries. Those with extensive experience and access to sufficient capital may head their own consulting firms.

Training for Careers in Brokerage and Investment Firms

Because securities sales representatives must be well informed about economic conditions and trends, a college education is increasingly important, especially in the larger securities firms. In fact, the overwhelming majority of workers in this occupation are college graduates. Although employers seldom require specialized academic training, courses in business administration, economics, and finance are helpful.

Many employers consider personal qualities and skills more important than academic training. Employers seek applicants who have sales ability and good communication skills, are well groomed, and possess a strong desire to succeed. Self-confidence and an ability to handle frequent rejections also are important ingredients for success.

Because maturity and the ability to work independently also are important, many employers prefer to hire those who have achieved success in other jobs. Some firms prefer candidates with sales experience, particularly those who have worked on commission in areas such as real estate or insurance. Therefore, most entrants to this occupation transfer from other jobs. Some begin working as securities sales representatives following retirement from other fields.

Securities sales representatives must meet state licensing requirements, which generally include passing an examination and, in some cases, furnishing a personal bond. In addition, sales representatives must register as representatives of their firm according to regulations of the securities exchanges where they do business or the National Association of Securities Dealers, Inc. (NASD).

Before beginners can qualify as registered representatives, they must pass the General Securities Registered Representative Examination, administered by the NASD, and be an employee of a registered firm for at least four months. Most states require a second examination—the Uniform Securities Agents State Law Examination. These tests measure the prospective representative's knowledge of the securities business, customer protection requirements, and record-keeping procedures. Many take correspondence courses in preparation for the securities examinations.

Most employers provide on-the-job training to help securities sales representatives meet the requirements for registration. In most firms, the training period generally takes about four months. Trainees in large firms may receive classroom instruction in securities analysis, effective speaking, and the finer points of selling; take courses offered by business schools and associations; and undergo a period of on-the-job training lasting up to two years.

Many firms like to rotate their trainees among various departments in the firm to give them a broader perspective of the securities business. In small firms, sales representatives generally receive training in outside institutions and on the job.

Securities sales representatives must understand the basic characteristics of a wide variety of financial products offered by brokerage firms. Representatives periodically take training, through their firms or outside institutions, to keep abreast of new financial products as they are introduced on the market and to improve their sales techniques. Training in the use of computers is important, as the securities sales business is highly automated.

The principal form of advancement for securities sales representatives is an increase in the number and size of the accounts they handle. Although beginners usually service the accounts of individual investors, eventually they may handle very large institutional accounts such as those of banks and pension funds. Some experienced sales representatives become branch office managers and supervise other sales representatives while continuing to provide services for their own customers. A few representatives advance to top management positions or become partners in their firms.

Banks and other credit institutions prefer to hire college graduates for financial services sales jobs. A business administration degree with a specialization in finance or a liberal arts degree including courses in accounting, economics, and marketing serves as excellent preparation for this job.

Financial services sales representatives learn through on-the-job training under the supervision of bank officers. Outstanding performance can lead to promotion to managerial positions.

Some brokerage clerk entrants are college graduates with degrees in business, finance, or the liberal arts. Some brokerage firms have a set plan of advancement that tracks college graduates from entry-level clerk jobs into management positions. These workers may start at higher salaries and advance more rapidly than those without a degree.

SAMPLE JOB ADVERTISEMENTS

To give you an idea of the kind of positions available, examine the sample job announcements in Exhibits 13.1 through 13.8. (Contact information is not provided here because these particular positions have already been filled.)

Exhibit 13.1

Economist Announcement

Job Title: International financial analyst (economist)

Location: Washington, D.C., and Africa

Description: We have an immediate need for a consultant to fill the position of international financial analyst. The consultant will be required to support international projects in multiple African countries. Position responsibilities will include budget formulation, acquisition planning, schedule development, performance monitoring, and system engineering.

Qualifications: Must have 10+ years' financial and/or budget analysis experience. Doctorate degree in related field required, along with strong analytical and quantitative skills, proficiency in Excel, and effective oral and written communication skills. Cost-benefit analysis with modeling background preferred. Experience within the aeronautical field a plus. Must be familiar with the operations of international lending institutions and must have the ability to recommend financing alternatives to clients. The position will be headquartered in Washington, D.C., with travel to Mozambique.

Exhibit 13.2

Lead Revenue Reporting Analyst Announcement

Job Title: Lead revenue reporting analyst

Location: California

Description: The position will establish and maintain monthly and weekly reporting and forecasting schedules; support operational and business development management with regular revenue forecasts (daily/weekly/monthly); prepare and present analysis of revenue trends and variances; ensure seamless incorporation of revenue reports and forecasts in overall financial planning documents and the annual business plan; and review and present studies on revenue trends and anomalies for use by operations and

continued

continued

business development personnel involved in maximizing system usage. The position will provide leadership to one or more junior analysts in accomplishing these tasks.

Qualifications: This position requires a B.S. in economics, business, finance, accounting, or a related discipline. M.B.A./C.P.A. a plus. Successful candidates will have at least five years' experience in financial analysis and/or revenue planning and forecasting, with at least two years' experience in a leadership role. At least two years' experience in a telecommunications environment or on-line services billing (especially wholesale) or other automated revenue/accounting system and/or budget/revenue variance analysis is a plus. Demonstrated verbal and written communications skills are required.

Exhibit 13.3

Financial Analyst Announcement

Job Title: Financial analyst (industrial)

Location: Georgia

Description: Position includes general accounting functions and contract/cost analysis. Included in the duties are general and subsidiary ledger preparation, customer billings, accounts receivable and accounts payable, fixed assets, expense report auditing, benefits accounting, budget development, rate analysis and job order/charging instructions.

Qualifications: B.S./B.A. in economics, accounting, or related financial field (M.B.A./C.P.A. preferred). Familiarity with Federal Acquisition Regulations and Cost Accounting Standards is desired.

Exhibit 13.4

Director Announcement

Job Title: Director, Personal Choice Retirement Product manager

Location: New York

Description: Leading discount brokerage house has a position responsible for the management and supervision of Personal Choice Retirement Product (PCRP). Includes the following: understanding and analysis of all our systems used to service the product, ability to forecast staffing and capacity planning for the product, supervise and work in partnership with sales and relationship management, leverage our knowledge to impact non-RPS servicing issues, work with RPS Marketing in the development of communications and collateral as needed, and develop and manage the reporting of financial information and metrics to senior management. Ultimately, provide product expertise and vision for product life cycle planning.

Qualification: Understanding of the retirement plan industry and the Personal Choice Retirement Product is required. Knowledge of our retail products, the retail business, retail segmentation strategies, and retail economics is necessary. Ability to understand, create, and present financial information is a must. Ability to work with cross-enterprise and cross-functional issues. Previous involvement in sales, customer segmentation, and pricing issues is desired. Strong desire to work in a demanding, change-oriented environment. Need to be action oriented, have a strong ability to deal with ambiguity, have a strong retail customer focus, and the ability to manage through roadblocks.

Exhibit 13.5

Investment Analyst Announcement

Job Title: Investment analyst (entry level)

Location: Illinois

Description: Self-starter needed for busy back office investment company. Duties include performance measurement and some phone interaction with clients.

Qualifications: B.S. in finance/accounting/economics. Strong Excel a must. Oracle a plus.

Exhibit 13.6

Senior Financial Analyst Announcement

Job Title: Senior financial analyst

Location: Miami, Florida

Description: High-growth company considering acquisitions needs strong analyst to review proforma projections and cash flow statements. Involvement with Due Diligence review of financial data.

Qualifications: B.S. in accounting/finance or economics. Five or more years' hands-on experience. Excellent analytical skills, communication, and managerial skills a must. Big 5 accounting background/C.P.A. preferred. Knowledge of spreadsheet software including Lotus or Excel.

Exhibit 13.7

Financial Planning Manager Announcement

Job Title: Financial planning manager

Location: New Orleans, Louisiana

Description: Prepare LRSP and AOP. Measure performance monthly. Responsible for monthly reporting. DCAA interface with compliance.

Qualifications: B.S., M.S. desired in economics. Hyperion experience (consolidated reporting). Budget, LSRP experience. Need broad accounting knowledge of G/L and income statement analysis. General ledger experience through consolidation.

Exhibit 13.8

Reporting and Analysis Specialist Announcement

Job Title: Global reporting and analysis specialist

Location: Massachusetts

Description: Imagine what you could accomplish at a leading global management and technology consulting organization that helps companies align strategy with people, process, and technology. Right now we're looking for a professional who can help us manage our financial processes. This professional will be responsible for analyzing and reporting the financial status of our local business unit and executing annual financial processes and recommending and implementing financial policies and processes across a large and geographically dispersed finance team, ensuring compliance with the internal policies and adherence to budgets.

Responsibilities:

- Prepare ad hoc analysis and financial reports, forecasts, and presentations for management approval

- Execute annual financial operating plan and January and April forecasts and processes

- Analyze financial/operational data and key performance indicators, highlight and understand variances, and improve analysis methodologies

- Provide support, coordinate activities, and issue resolutions to finance team as needed

- Assist in the development of continuous improvement initiatives; provide leverage to broader finance team to avoid redundancies

- Supervise and develop analysts' roles

Qualifications:

- Six to eight years' experience in a finance role, including at least one year of supervisory experience

- Bachelor's degree, preferably in economics, finance, or accounting

- Thorough knowledge of accounting principles and financial analysis

- Excellent oral and written communication and interpersonal skills

continued

continued

- Ability to interact well with all levels of executives and to facilitate resolutions across multiple work groups

- Strong organizational skills; ability to prioritize multiple requests from various audiences in fast-paced working environment

- High degree of independence and flexibility; enthusiastic attitude and strong teamwork ethic

- Familiarity with business software packages (Microsoft Word, Excel, PowerPoint, or equivalent)

SALARIES

Bank Teller

In a recent survey, median annual earnings of full-time tellers were $16,300. The lowest 10 percent earned less than $11,900, while the top 10 percent earned more than $24,800. Some banks offer incentives, whereby tellers earn supplemental rewards for inducing customers to use other financial products and services offered by the bank. In general, greater responsibilities result in a higher salary. Experience, length of service, and, especially, the location and size of the bank also are important.

Part-time tellers generally do not receive typical benefits, such as life and health insurance.

Loan Officer

The form of compensation for loan officers varies, depending on the lending institution. Some banks offer salary plus commission as an incentive to increase the number of loans processed, while others pay only salaries.

According to a salary survey conducted by Robert Half International, a staffing services firm specializing in accounting and finance, residential real estate mortgage loan officers earn between $30,600 and $45,000; commercial real estate mortgage loan officers earn between $45,100 and $73,000; consumer loan officers earn between $28,900 and $48,000; and commercial lenders earn between $37,400 and $85,000.

Smaller banks generally paid 15 percent less than larger banks. Loan officers who are paid on a commission basis generally earn more than those on salary only.

Banks and other lenders sometimes offer their loan officers free checking privileges and somewhat lower interest rates on personal loans.

Financial Manager

The median annual salary of financial managers is approximately $42,000. The lowest 10 percent earn $21,800 or less, while the top 10 percent earn more than $81,100.

According to another survey by Robert Half International, salaries of assistant controllers range from $41,000 in the smallest firms to $81,000 in the largest firms; controllers earn between $47,000 and $138,000; and chief financial officers/treasurers earn between $62,000 and $307,000.

The results of the Treasury Management Association's 1997 compensation survey are presented in the table below. The earnings listed in the table represent total compensation, including bonuses. The survey also found that financial managers with a master's degree in business administration average $10,900 more than managers with a bachelor's degree.

Annual Earnings for Selected Financial Managers, 1997	
Chief financial officer	$142,900
Vice president of finance	$138,000
Treasurer	$122,500
Assistant treasurer	$88,400
Controller	$85,100
Treasury manager	$66,900
Assistant controller	$56,200
Senior analyst	$55,600
Cash manager	$51,600
Analyst	$40,500
Assistant cash manager	$38,800

Source: Treasury Management Association

Salary level depends upon the manager's experience and the size and location of the organization and is likely to be higher in larger organizations and cities. Many financial managers in private industry receive additional compensation in the form of bonuses, which also vary substantially by the size of the firm.

Securities and Financial Services Sales Representatives

Median annual earnings of securities and financial services sales representatives are approximately $38,800; the middle 50 percent earn between

$24,300 and $73,500. Ten percent earn less than $18,100, and 10 percent earn more than $98,400.

On average, financial services sales representatives earn considerably less than securities sales representatives.

Trainees usually are paid an hourly wage or salary, until they meet licensing and registration requirements. After candidates are licensed and registered, their earnings depend on commissions from the sale or purchase of stocks and bonds, life insurance, or other securities for customers. Commission earnings are likely to be high when there is much buying and selling and low when there is a slump in market activity.

Most firms provide sales representatives with a steady income by paying a "draw against commission"—a minimum salary based on commissions that they can be expected to earn. Securities sales representatives who can provide their clients with the most complete financial services should enjoy the greatest income stability.

Financial services sales representatives usually are paid a salary; some receive a bonus if they meet certain established goals.

Salaries for Brokerage Clerks

Salaries for brokerage clerks vary considerably, depending upon the region of the country and the size of the firm. The median salary falls just above $25,000 per year.

CAREER OUTLOOK

Bank Teller

Little or no change in employment of bank tellers is expected through 2006. Nevertheless, many job openings will arise from replacement needs because the occupation is large and turnover is high, which is characteristic of occupations that generally require little formal education and offer relatively low pay. Applicants for part-time jobs should fare better than applicants for full-time jobs.

Banks are expected to decline in number and increase in size as interstate banking grows. As banks become larger, the operations, duties and responsibilities, and staffing of branch offices will change. To cut costs, banks are likely to increasingly shift from employing full-time tellers to part-time tellers. Banks also have branches inside supermarkets and department stores; instead of tellers, many have ATMs and more highly trained customer service representatives, who can perform the standard duties of tellers, as well as open new accounts and arrange for customers to receive other services or products the bank provides.

Banks also are increasingly using technology to cut costs. For example, some banks have introduced branches that consist entirely of ATMs and kiosks. Kiosks use ATM technology and video screens and cameras to allow customers at several remote locations to conduct transactions with tellers at a central location. Some banks also allow banking by computer and by telephone.

Loan Officer and Counselor

While employment in banks, where most loan officers and counselors are found, is projected to decline, employment of loan officers and counselors is expected to grow faster than the average for all occupations through 2006. As the population and economy grow, applications for commercial, consumer, and mortgage loans will increase, spurring demand for loan officers and counselors. Growth in the variety and complexity of loans, and the importance of loan officers to the success of banks and other lending institutions, also should assure employment growth. Although increased demand will generate many new jobs, most openings will result from the need to replace workers who leave the occupation or retire. College graduates and those with banking, lending, or sales experience should have the best job prospects.

Loan officers and counselors are less likely to lose their jobs than other workers in banks and other lending institutions during economic downturns. Because loans are the major source of income for banks, loan officers are fundamental to the success of their organizations. Also, many loan officers are compensated in part on a commission basis. Loan counselors are likely to see an increase in the number of delinquent loans during difficult economic times.

Financial Manager

Like other managerial occupations, the number of applicants for financial management positions is expected to exceed the number of openings, resulting in competition for jobs. Those with lending experience and familiarity with the latest lending regulations and financial products and services should enjoy the best opportunities for branch management jobs in banks. Those with a graduate degree, a strong analytical background, and knowledge of various aspects of financial management, such as asset management and information and technology management, should enjoy the best opportunities for other financial management positions. Developing expertise in a rapidly growing industry, such as health care, could also be an advantage in the job market.

Employment of financial managers is expected to increase about as fast as the average for all occupations through 2006. The need for skilled financial management will increase due to the demands of global trade, the proliferation of complex financial instruments, and changing federal and state laws and regulations. Many firms have reduced the ranks of middle managers in an effort to be more efficient and competitive, but much of the downsizing and restructuring is complete. The banking industry, on the other hand, is still undergoing mergers and consolidation and may eliminate some financial management positions as a result.

Securities Sales Representative

Because of the highly competitive nature of securities sales work, many beginners leave the occupation because they are unable to establish a sufficient clientele. Once established, however, securities sales representatives have a very strong attachment to their occupation because of high earnings and the considerable investment in training.

The demand for securities sales representatives fluctuates as the economy expands and contracts. Thus, in an economic downturn the number of people seeking jobs usually exceeds the number of openings—sometimes by a great deal. Even during periods of rapid economic expansion, competition for securities sales training positions—particularly in larger firms—is keen because of potentially high earnings.

Job opportunities for both securities and financial services sales representatives should be best for mature individuals with successful work experience. Opportunities for inexperienced sales representatives should be best in smaller firms.

Employment of securities sales representatives is expected to grow much faster than the average for all occupations through 2006 as economic growth, rising personal incomes, and greater inherited wealth increase the funds available for investment. As banks offer increasingly complex financial services, employment of financial services sales representatives should grow rapidly, even as overall employment in banking declines and more people conduct their banking from home via personal computer.

More individual investors are expected to purchase common stocks, mutual funds, and other financial products after seeking advice from securities sales representatives regarding the increasing array of investment alternatives. Deregulation has enabled brokerage firms to sell certificates of deposit, offer checking and deposit services through cash management accounts, and sell insurance products, such as annuities and life insurance. Growth in the number and size of institutional investors will be strong as more people enroll in pension plans, set up individual retirement accounts, establish trust funds, and contribute to the endowment funds of colleges and other nonprofit institutions. Additional representatives also will be needed to sell securities issued by new and expanding corporations, state and local governments financing public improvements, and foreign governments, whose securities have become attractive to U.S. investors, as international trade expands.

Investors increasingly rely on the growing number of financial planners to assist them in selecting the proper options among a wide variety of financial alternatives. In addition, demand should increase as banks and credit institutions expand the range of financial services they offer and issue more loans for personal and commercial use.

Brokerage Clerk

Employment of brokerage clerks is expected to grow about as fast as the average for all occupations through 2006. Employment of statement clerks is projected to decline. Nevertheless, some jobs will become available each year to replace brokerage and statement clerks who transfer to other occupations or leave the labor force.

CLOSE-UPS

J. DOUGLAS NOBLES, LOAN OFFICER/PRESIDENT

J. Douglas Nobles has worked with the Mortgage Shop, a branch of Lamar Bank in Hattiesburg, Mississippi, since 1997. Before that, he worked as the manager/loan officer of United Companies Financial Corporation in Hattiesburg for seventeen years. He has been in the loan business since 1975.

Getting Started

"I started out in this business collecting loan payments. I've always enjoyed helping people, and in banking you're able to provide much-needed assistance to your customers.

"Certain fields are right for certain people, and banking has always been something that I enjoyed doing.

"I went from collecting to assistant manager and loan officer of United Companies Financial Corporation, where I eventually ran the Hattiesburg office for seventeen years as manager/loan officer.

continued

continued

"Basically, I received my training on the job, learning from experts in the field, making mistakes and learning how to correct them, and so forth.

"With a B.S., or even an M.S. degree, you still will receive the majority of your training in this business on the job. Each bank does things a little differently, and each type of loan is handled a little differently. It's a matter of working on the job to learn the differences.

"Of course, attending banking seminars is very helpful too. The banking industry is excellent about providing periodic training in new banking laws and procedures, and I've been to numerous ones through the years in Baton Rouge, Louisiana; Atlanta, Georgia; Jackson, Mississippi; and more.

"Many banks provide an on-the-job training program for officers for six to eight weeks when just beginning. Those programs basically walk a new officer through each and every branch of the bank to give them a good overall view of the bank itself."

What the Work Is Like

"My main duty is to help people who are financially stressed to work out solutions to get them back in good financial standing. I help them lower their total financial obligations by using equity in their home, or reduce their payments to where they can better handle their obligations.

"I spend a lot of time on the phone and talking to people in the office. I take credit applications, spend time on the road looking at different properties that people want to borrow money on, and so forth. I call on various lenders that don't do the type of business that we do to get them to refer their business to us. Also, I deal with investors and bank officials every day. The job is basically a sales job—selling the loan packages that we have in order to help someone out of a financial bind.

"The work comes and goes. Sometimes, it's extremely busy and hectic, and we work long hours. Other times, it's laid-back with not much going on. During those times, we work on soliciting new business or completing paperwork. But the work goes in spurts—it's the nature of the business.

"Being a loan officer is very interesting. There are a lot of different things you can do to generate business in your slow times, and you must be creative to loan people the money they need. You have to look at their whole financial situation and see if you can come up with a payment that will best fit their needs that they can afford.

"There is a lot of paperwork in this business, but I really don't mind. I guess I've gotten used to it, and it's part of the job.

"I work at least forty hours a week, sometimes more during busy times. The atmosphere in my office is relaxed. The people in the office enjoy coming to work. We all get along, have a good time, and make sure the job gets done.

"Some banks make you feel that they are too important to talk to you and too important to help you out. We don't do that. We try to make our customers feel they are very important. By doing so, they'll recommend us to other customers, and they'll come back when they need more financial assistance. You have to be personable and friendly in this business to make it.

"The thing I like most about this job is helping people. It's extremely gratifying to get someone back on their feet financially and to help them turn their lives around. I've been in this business long enough to know the different ways to help them, and it's always a challenge to work with customers from all types of backgrounds. I enjoy helping people out of a financial bind and getting them started to where they can pay their bills.

"The thing I like least is not being able to find an investor who will buy a loan for a customer and eventually having to turn the customer down. It's very tough having to turn someone down for a loan. It's hard to send them out the door when I can't help them, to watch the sad expressions on their faces and their reactions to the news.

"Starting salaries for this part of the country depend on each lender. Someone just starting out in the field could expect to earn between $18,000 and $24,000 a year, plus commissions. The starting salaries are based on a minimum monthly salary plus a commission off loans originated. Loan officers earn a 30 percent commission on the points—the fee the bank charges for the loan.

continued

continued

"Some institutions will pay a straight salary with no commissions, and other institutions will pay a straight commission based on loans originated. It all depends on the lender."

Advice from J. Douglas Nobles

"To be in this business, you must have a good personality. You must be friendly, willing to spend time with your customers and make them feel at ease. You have to be able to listen to people's problems and sympathize with them.

"To get in the business, I suggest getting a B.S. degree in banking and finance or banking and real estate. Have a good strong knowledge of the banking and real estate industries.

"Be prepared to start at the bottom, work hard, and work your way up. Learn as much as you can. Listen to the experts in the field. Be friendly to everyone you meet. You never know when that person might need your help.

"Get on the level of your customers—don't give them the impression that you're too 'good' to talk to them. You'll never get business that way. Instead, become their friend. You'll spend a lot of time talking, but in the end, it will pay off."

RICHARD G. LEADER, EXECUTIVE DIRECTOR, INSTITUTIONAL SALES

Richard G. Leader is an executive director with CIBC Oppenheimer, an investment broker in Houston, Texas. He earned a B.A. from Wake Forest in Winston-Salem, North Carolina, in 1970 and an M.B.A. from Vanderbilt in Nashville, Tennessee, in 1976. He is also a CFA (Chartered Financial Analyst) and has been working in the field since 1983.

Getting Started

"I started investing a small amount of savings from my paper route in the stock market at age twelve. My first stock went up 50 percent in a year, and I've been hooked ever since.

"Because of general family interest in the market, I continued to follow the market, even when I had blown all my profits on my first car. My mother took me to an annual meeting of General Motors at age fourteen, and this included a factory tour that I found fascinating and memorable. This made me realize that stocks represent interests in real operating businesses, not just meaningless or speculative price quotes.

"To get my first job, I went through the normal M.B.A. recruiting routine. I wrote proposal letters to about fifty Wall Street firms in my final year of my M.B.A. program and got invited to interview by a few. I went to New York for several days of interviews, got three offers, and accepted an offer from Citibank's Investment Management Group for $20,000 in 1976, which was the highest salary offered to any Vanderbilt graduate student that year.

"Citibank transferred me to Houston, and then I went to work for Drexel Burnham. After they went bankrupt, I knew I wanted to stay in Houston so I called around town to other firms and got a $50,000 up-front offer for six months at Rotan Mosely, which has since shut down its operation.

"Since then, I've been with Oppenheimer, a job I also got through phone calls and interviews."

What the Work Is Like

"Institutional equity sales means selling a brokerage firm's products and services to professional money managers, such as mutual funds, pension, and retirement funds. Anyone with a few million dollars, even wealthy individuals, might qualify as an 'institution.'

"I am constantly looking for information or ideas that will 'beat the market.' If you can't beat the market, you might as well buy an index.

"Ideas usually come from one of our industry analysts, who are supposed experts in areas of business such as autos, aluminum, semiconductors, and telecommunications. We get information that our analyst believes to be correct, such as improved earnings prospects for a company (i.e., Ford), we try to convince people to buy large quantities of that stock through us, and we earn a commission. If we are right more often than wrong, our clients gain confidence in our suggestions, and will do more and more business with us over time.

continued

continued

"In addition to our research sales we also sell new issues of public stock, or IPOs—initial public offerings. This can be extraordinarily easy or difficult depending on market conditions and how popular or hot an industry might be. For example, a recent IPO for an Internet company was up 100 percent the very first day. That was an easy sale—we really 'gave' that stock to only our very best customers.

"I earn around $300,000 a year on a 100 percent commission basis. When you first join a firm, you have a small customer base based on cold calls or family. As your customer base increases and as their assets increase, your commission increases as well. Some firms will give a base salary for a year or two for their beginning salespeople—which is modest at best, $25,000 a year or so.

"The pace is quick, the competition is very intense. Most big institutions deal with twenty-five or more brokers, each trying to have his or her voice heard over the others. If you are viewed as someone with good money-making ideas, clients pay you back handsomely.

"I enjoy the constant change; figuring out what's 'real,' what's unimportant, what the next money-making opportunity is. These are the things that are exciting about my job.

"The downside is playing politics with the management in New York City."

Advice from Richard G. Leader

"Learn how to sell something first. The same principles apply. Be genuinely interested in business and finance. You must be somewhat entrepreneurial and willing to take risks."

CHAPTER FOURTEEN

PATH 5: TEACHING

*T*hose who can, do; those who can, also teach. Many economists prefer to share their knowledge in the classroom rather than work in the field. Others, after a stint in government or the private sector, choose to finish their careers in an academic environment.

DEFINITION OF THE CAREER PATH

There are four main settings in which economics teachers usually work: secondary schools, community colleges, four-year colleges and universities, and adult education programs.

Secondary Schools
In many U.S. states and in Canada, economics is integrated throughout the curriculum from kindergarten through twelfth grade. Most school districts offer specific economics courses at the high school level.

Community Colleges
Most community colleges offer courses in economics; some offer economics as a major for an associate's degree. Credits are usually transferable to a four-year college or university.

Four-Year Colleges and Universities
The majority of economics courses are offered in four-year colleges and universities. Job positions range from instructor to full professor, with some programs hiring research assistants as well.

Adult Education Programs

University evening and extension programs often offer economics as part of the curriculum. Instructors can be hired from the pool of day faculty or drawn from economists working in the field.

RESPONSIBILITIES

In today's classrooms, economics teachers are using more props or sophisticated manipulatives, such as computers, cameras, tape recorders, films, slides, overhead projectors, telecommunication systems, and videodiscs to help students understand abstract concepts, solve problems, and facilitate critical thinking.

Classes are becoming less structured, and students are working in groups to discuss and solve problems together. Preparing students for the future workforce is the major stimulus generating the changes in education. To be prepared, students must be able to interact with others, adapt to new technology, and logically think through problems. Teachers provide the tools and environment for their students to develop these skills.

Teachers observe and evaluate a student's performance and potential. Teachers increasingly are using new assessment methods, such as examining a portfolio of a student's graph work or writing to measure student achievement. Teachers assess the portfolio at the end of a learning period to judge a student's overall progress. They may then provide additional assistance in areas where a student may need help.

Seeing students develop new skills and gain an appreciation of the joy of learning can be very rewarding. However, teaching may be frustrating when dealing with unmotivated and disrespectful students.

This is not usually the case at the college level, however. Students register for economics courses because it is a subject they are interested in, not required to take.

College faculty usually spend fewer hours in the classroom than secondary school teachers do, but they have as many meetings, if not more, and they must be available for office hours to meet with students who need help.

College faculty are often responsible for guiding students, at both undergraduate and graduate levels, supervising course selection, theses, and dissertation projects.

Research and writing for scholarly journals is often a large part of a college professor's routine. This is less so at the community college level. Achieving substantial publications is usually a prerequisite for promotion, a professorship, and tenure.

THE QUALIFICATIONS YOU'LL NEED

Aspiring secondary school teachers either major in the subject they plan to teach while also taking education courses, or major in education and take subject courses. Some states require a master's degree for permanent teacher certification.

More often than not, a Ph.D. degree is required for teaching at the college level, both at four-year and two-year community colleges. However, some community colleges will hire instructors with a master's degree.

If you are interested in a career in college teaching but are concerned by the additional costs of graduate school, you shouldn't let that deter you. The vast majority of students in Ph.D. programs in economics receive assistantships or fellowships that cover the cost of tuition and provide an annual income of $6,000 to $10,000 per year.

CAREER OUTLOOK

Secondary Schools

The job market for teachers varies widely by geographic area and by subject specialty. Many inner cities—characterized by high crime rates, high poverty rates, and overcrowded conditions—and rural areas—characterized by their remote location and relatively low salaries—have difficulty attracting enough teachers, so job prospects should continue to be better in these areas than in suburban districts.

Currently, many school districts have difficulty hiring qualified teachers in some subjects—economics, mathematics, science (especially chemistry and physics), bilingual education, and computer science. Specialties that currently have an abundance of qualified teachers include general elementary education, English, art, physical education, and social studies. Teachers who are geographically mobile and who obtain licensure in more than one subject should have a distinct advantage in finding a job.

With enrollments of minorities increasing, coupled with a shortage of minority teachers, efforts to recruit minority teachers should intensify. Also, the number of non-English-speaking students has grown dramatically, especially in California and Florida, which have large Spanish-speaking student populations, creating demand for bilingual teachers and those who teach English as a second language (ESL).

Overall employment of secondary school teachers is expected to increase about as fast as the average for all occupations through 2006. The expected retirement of a large number of teachers currently in their forties and fifties should open up many additional jobs.

Assuming relatively little change in average class size, employment growth of teachers depends on population growth rates and corresponding student enrollments. Enrollment of fourteen- to seventeen-year-olds is expected to grow through 2006.

The number of teachers employed is also dependent on state and local expenditures for education. Pressures from taxpayers to limit spending could result in fewer teachers than projected; pressures to spend more to improve the quality of education could increase the teacher workforce.

The supply of teachers also is expected to increase in response to reports of improved job prospects, more teacher involvement in school policy, and greater public interest in education.

In recent years, the total number of bachelor's and master's degrees granted in education has steadily increased. In addition, more teachers will be drawn from a reserve pool of career changers, substitute teachers, and teachers completing alternative certification programs, relocating to different schools, and reentering the workforce.

Colleges and Universities

Employment of college and university faculty is expected to increase about as fast as the average for all occupations through 2006 as enrollments in higher education increase. Many additional openings will arise as faculty members retire. Faculty retirements should increase significantly from the late 1990s through 2006 as a large number of faculty who entered the profession during the 1950s and 1960s reach retirement age. Most faculty members likely to retire are full-time tenured professors.

However, in an effort to cut costs some institutions are expected to either leave these positions vacant or hire part-time, nontenured faculty as replacements. Prospective job applicants should be prepared to face keen competition for available jobs as growing numbers of Ph.D. graduates, including foreign-born graduates, vie for fewer full-time openings. As more and more Ph.D.s compete for openings, master's degree holders may find competition for jobs even more intense.

Enrollments in institutions of higher education increased in the mid-1980s through the early 1990s despite a decline in the traditional college-age (eighteen to twenty-four) population. This resulted from a higher proportion of eighteen- to twenty-four-year-olds attending college, along with a growing number of part-time, female, and older students. Between 1996 and 2006, the traditional college-age population will begin to grow again, spurred by the leading edge of the baby-boom "echo" generation (children of the baby boomers) reaching college age. College enrollment is projected to rise from fourteen million in 1996 to sixteen million in 2006, an increase of 14 percent.

In the past two decades, keen competition for faculty jobs forced some applicants to accept part-time or short-term academic appointments that offered little hope of tenure and forced others to seek nonacademic positions. This trend of hiring adjunct or part-time faculty is likely to continue because of financial difficulties faced by colleges and universities. Many colleges, faced with reduced state funding for higher education, have increased the hiring of part-time faculty to save money on pay and benefits.

Public two-year colleges employ a significantly higher number of part-time faculty as a percentage of their total staff than public four-year colleges and universities, but all institutions have increased their part-time hiring. With uncertainty over future funding, many colleges and universities are continuing to cut costs by eliminating some academic programs, increasing class size, and closely monitoring all expenses.

Once enrollments and retirements start increasing at a faster pace in the early 2000s, opportunities for college faculty may begin to improve somewhat. Growing numbers of students will necessitate hiring more faculty to teach. At the same time, many faculty will be retiring, opening up even more positions.

Job prospects will continue to be better in certain fields—economics, business, engineering, health science, and computer science, for example—that offer attractive nonacademic job opportunities and attract fewer applicants for academic positions.

Employment of college faculty is affected by the nonacademic job market. Excellent job prospects in a field—for example, computer science—cause more students to enroll, increasing faculty needs in that field. On the other hand, poor job prospects in a field, such as history in recent years, discourage students and reduce demand for faculty.

SALARIES

Secondary Schools

According to the National Education Association (NEA), the estimated average salary of all public secondary school teachers is $38,600 a year. Private school teachers generally earn less than public school teachers. The NEA report reveals that the average teacher salary in America actually declined from the previous year by nearly half a percentage point when adjusted for inflation. The result: recruiting and retaining quality teachers will be more difficult than ever before.

One contributing factor, NEA researchers point out, is that younger teachers, who start at much lower salary levels, have begun replacing the first wave of retirees, which has the effect of reducing the average salary to some degree. Still, teachers as a profession lost ground to all other workers in the nation, whose salaries rose by nearly a full percentage point after inflation last year, according to the U.S. Department of Labor.

Bob Chase, president of the NEA, called the salary data a "disturbing development," since the U.S. Department of Education predicts a million new teachers need to be hired over the next seven years to meet rising enrollments and to replace the large number of teachers who will be retiring. "We'll need significant numbers of skilled, well-trained candidates to fill these vacancies," Chase said. "We'd better be offering competitive salaries if we expect to hire top-quality individuals."

"As important as teacher salaries are, there are other factors that can also help make teaching a more attractive profession," Chase added. "Smaller class sizes, safe schools and disciplined students, and high standards for the profession will also help attract and retain excellent teachers."

In some schools, teachers receive extra pay for coaching sports and working with students in extracurricular activities. Some teachers earn extra income during the summer working in the school system or in other jobs.

Rankings of the States, the report published each year since the 1960s by NEA Research, contains rank-ordered statistics for the fifty states and the District of Columbia. The report includes dozens of charts that researchers and education writers rely on throughout the year. In addition to data about teacher salaries, the report includes information on average per pupil expenditures, percentage of school costs borne by each level of government, per capita income, population, pupil-teacher ratios, and other factors affecting school resources and quality.

Copies of *Rankings of the States* can be ordered by calling (800) 229-4200 or by writing to:

NEA Professional Library
P.O. Box 2035
Annapolis Junction, MD 20701

Colleges and Universities

Earnings vary according to faculty rank and type of institution, geographic area, and field. According to a survey by the American Association of University Professors, salaries for full-time faculty average $51,000. By rank, the average for professors was $65,400; associate professors, $48,300; assistant professors, $40,100; instructors, $30,800; and lecturers, $33,700.

Faculty in four-year institutions earn higher salaries, on the average, than those in two-year schools. Average salaries for faculty in public institutions ($50,400) are generally lower than those for private independent schools ($57,500) but higher than those for religion-affiliated private institutions ($45,200).

In fields with high-paying nonacademic alternatives—notably medicine and law but also engineering, economics, and business, among others, earnings exceed these averages. In others, such as the humanities and education, they are lower.

Most faculty members have significant earnings in addition to their base salary, from consulting, teaching additional courses, research, writing for publication, or other employment, both during the academic year and during the summer.

Most college and university faculty enjoy some unique benefits, including access to campus facilities, tuition waivers for dependents, housing and travel allowances, and paid sabbatical leaves. Part-time faculty have fewer benefits than full-time faculty and usually do not receive health insurance, retirement benefits, or sabbatical leave.

SAMPLE JOB ADVERTISEMENTS

To get an idea of the kind of positions available, examine the sample teaching and research job announcements in Exhibits 14.1 through 14.5. (Contact information is not provided here because these particular positions have already been filled.)

Exhibit 14.1

Economics Announcement

Position: Economics instructor

Institution: College in Pennsylvania, Department of Economics

Duties: Teach micro and macro, other courses, plus normal faculty duties. Master's required, doctorate preferred. Requires commitment to Christian higher education and breadth of teaching skills. Send curriculum vitae, copies

continued

continued

of transcripts, letter addressing qualifications and philosophy of Christian higher education, and at least three references.

Exhibit 14.2

Research/Social Policy Announcement

Position: Research associate/social policy

Institution: Social research firm in California

Qualifications: A small business engaged in research and policy analysis of human service programs is seeking a research associate for full-time employment. Completion of graduate-level degree in the social sciences, including economics, sociology, education, public policy, health policy, psychology, or a related field plus several years' experience in quantitative and/or qualitative research preferred. Relevant research areas include workforce development, education, vocational training, human services, and related fields. Good writing skills, relevant research experience, and strong organizational skills are essential.

Duties: Duties will include a combination of the following: (1) design and conduct qualitative case study research based on telephone discussions and/or site visits to specific programs; (2) assist in the development, administration, and analysis of surveys of program administrators or participants; (3) assist in the collection, maintenance, and/or analysis of quantitative data on the participants, services, and outcomes of education, training, or other human service programs; and (4) help draft reports on evaluation findings. Salary range $45,000 to $60,000. Send resume and cover letter.

Exhibit 14.3

Teaching Announcement

Position: Teacher

Institution: International school in Cairo, Egypt

Description: American teachers needed to teach different subjects (English language, math, science, economics, or business/social studies). Starting salary $15,000 to $20,000 (American dollars) annually. Two and a half months' paid summer vacation, starting 15th June through end of August.

Exhibit 14.4

Research/Transportation Policy Announcement

Position: Researcher/transportation policy

Institution: University in Iowa

Description: Full-time permanent research position at a growing, progressive university research center. Ph.D. in economics, public policy, or planning preferred. Send curriculum vitae, cover letter, and discussion of research interests and experience.

Exhibit 14.5

Economics/Business Announcement

Position: Economics/business instructor

Institution: University in South Carolina

Description: Economics or business for adult undergraduate and graduate degree extension courses. Evening classes. Business or corporate experience desirable. Terminal degrees are preferred.

PROFESSIONAL ASSOCIATIONS

Professional associations and societies generally provide information on academic and nonacademic employment opportunities in their fields. Some offer newsletters and other periodicals and list job openings. Some have job placement services.

You can find addresses for professional associations for many academic disciplines in the *Encyclopedia of Associations*, available at your library. In addition, the Internet has become a valuable resource for information. Conduct a Web search using keywords such as *economics*, *careers*, *programs*, or *jobs*.

The following list includes websites where they are available. Often, with just a click of your mouse, you can request that information be sent to you.

General

American Agricultural Economics Association (AAEA)
415 S. Duff Ave., Ste. C
Ames, IA 50010-6600
http://www.aaea.org/staff.html

American Economic Association (AEA)
2014 Broadway, Ste. 305
Nashville, TN 37203
http://www.vanderbilt.edu/AEA/

Canadian Economics Association (CEA)
Lars Osberg
Dalhousie University

Department of Economics
Halifax, NS B3H 3J5
Canada
http://economics.ca/

Econometric Society
http://gemini.econ.yale.edu/es/

National Economic Association (NEA)
Dr. Alfred Edwards
School of Business Administration
University of Michigan
Ann Arbor, MI 48109-1234
http://www.ncat.edu/~neconasc/

Actuaries

American Academy of Actuaries
1100 17th St. NW, 7th Floor
Washington, DC 20036

American Society of Pension Actuaries
4350 N. Fairfax Dr., Ste. 820
Arlington, VA 22203

Casualty Actuarial Society
1100 N. Glebe Rd., Ste. 600
Arlington, VA 22201
http://www.casact.org

Society of Actuaries
475 N. Martingale Rd., Ste. 800
Schaumburg, IL 60173-2226

Banking, Finance, and Investment

State bankers' associations can furnish specific information about job opportunities in their states. Or you can contact individual banks to inquire about job openings and to obtain more details about the activities, responsibilities, and preferred qualifications of tellers.

General information about tellers and other banking occupations (such as loan officers and loan counselors), training opportunities, and the banking industry is available from

American Bankers Association
1120 Connecticut Ave. NW
Washington, DC 20036

For information about financial management careers, contact

American Bankers Association
1120 Connecticut Ave. NW
Washington, DC 20036

Financial Management Association, International
College of Business Administration
University of South Florida
Tampa, FL 33620-5500

For information about financial careers in business credit management; the Credit Business Associate, Credit Business Fellow, and Certified Credit Executive programs; and institutions offering graduate courses in credit and financial management, contact

National Association of Credit Management (NACM)
Credit Research Foundation
8815 Centre Park Dr.
Columbia, MD 21045-2117
http://www.nacm.org/

For information about careers in treasury management, from entry level to chief financial officer, and the Certified Cash Manager and Certified Treasury Executive programs, contact

Treasury Management Association
7315 Wisconsin Ave., Ste. 600 West
Bethesda, MD 20814

For information about the Chartered Financial Analyst program, contact

Association for Investment Management and Research
5 Boar's Head Ln.
P.O. Box 3668
Charlottesville, VA 22903
http://www.aimr.com/

For information about financial management careers in the health care industry, contact

Healthcare Financial Management Association
Two Westbrook Corporate Center, Ste. 700
Westchester, IL 60154

Information about job opportunities for securities sales representatives may be obtained from the personnel departments of individual securities firms.

For information about job opportunities for financial services sales representatives in various states, contact state bankers' associations.

Business

National Association of Business Economists (NABE)
1233 20th St. NW, #505
Washington, DC 20036
http://www.nabe.com/

Education

The National Education Association (NEA) is the nation's largest professional employee organization, representing more than 2.3 million elementary and secondary teachers, higher-education faculty, education support personnel, school administrators, retired educators, and students preparing to become teachers.

National Education Association
1201 16th St. NW
Washington, DC 20036

National Association of Economic Educators (NAEE)
Nebraska Council on Economic Education
339 College of Business Administration
University of Nebraska–Lincoln
Lincoln, NE 68588-0404
http://ecedweb.unomaha.edu/naee.htm

A list of institutions with teacher education programs accredited by the National Council for Accreditation of Teacher Education can be obtained from

National Council for Accreditation of Teacher Education
2010 Massachusetts Ave. NW, 2nd Floor
Washington, DC 20036

For information on voluntary teacher certification requirements, contact

National Board for Professional Teaching Standards
300 River Pl.
Detroit, MI 48207

High School Teaching

Information on certification requirements and approved teacher training institutions is available from local school systems and state departments of education.

Information on teachers' unions and education-related issues may be obtained from

American Federation of Teachers
555 New Jersey Ave. NW
Washington, DC 20001

American Association of Colleges for Teacher Education
One Dupont Circle NW, Suite 610
Washington, DC 20036

National Association of Independent Schools
75 Federal St.
Boston, MA 02110

College and University Teaching

For information on college teaching careers, contact

American Association of University Professors
1012 14th St. NW
Washington, DC 20005

Government

Information on obtaining a job with the federal government may be obtained from the Office of Personnel Management through a telephone-based system. Consult your telephone directory under *U.S. Government* for a local number or call (912) 757-3000 (TDD 912-744-2299). That number is not toll free and charges may result. Information also is available from their Internet site: http://www.usajobs.opm.gov/. See Chapter 10 for more information.

Health Care

American College of Healthcare Executives
One N. Franklin St., Ste. 1700
Chicago, IL 60606
http://www.ache.org

Information about undergraduate and graduate academic programs in health administration is available from

Association of University Programs in Health Administration
1911 N. Fort Myer Dr., Ste. 503
Arlington, VA 22209
http://www.aupha.org

For a list of accredited graduate programs in health services administration, contact

Accrediting Commission on Education for Health Services Administration
1911 N. Fort Myer Dr., Ste. 503
Arlington, VA 22209

For information about career opportunities in long-term care administration, contact

American College of Health Care Administrators
325 S. Patrick St.
Alexandria, VA 22314

For information about career opportunities in medical group practices and ambulatory care management, contact

Medical Group Management Association
104 Inverness Terrace East
Englewood, CO 80112

History

Economic History Association (EHA)
Department of Economics
213 Summerfield Hall
University of Kansas
Lawrence, KS 66045
http://www.eh.net/EHA/

Human Resources

For information about careers in employee training and development, contact

American Society for Training and Development
1640 King St.
Box 1443
Alexandria, VA 22313

For information about careers and certification in employee compensation and benefits, contact

American Compensation Association
14040 Northsight Blvd.
Scottsdale, AZ 85260

Information about careers and certification in employee benefits is available from

International Foundation of Employee Benefit Plans
18700 W. Bluemound Rd.
Brookfield, WI 53045

For information about careers in arbitration and other aspects of dispute resolution, contact

American Arbitration Association
140 W. 51st St.
New York, NY 10020

For information about academic programs in industrial relations, contact

Industrial Relations Research Association
University of Wisconsin
7226 Social Science Bldg.
1180 Observatory Dr.
Madison, WI 53706

Information about personnel careers in the health care industry is available from

American Society for Healthcare
Human Resources Administration
One N. Franklin, 31st Floor
Chicago, IL 60606

For information about personnel and labor relations careers in government, contact

International Association of Personnel in Employment Security
1801 Louisville Rd.
Frankfort, KY 40601

Insurance

General information about an insurance underwriter career is available from the home offices of many life insurance and property-liability insurance companies. Information about the insurance business in general and the underwriting function in particular also may be obtained from

The American Institute for Chartered Property and Casualty Underwriters and the Insurance Institute of America
720 Providence Rd.
P.O. Box 3016
Malvern, PA 19355-0716

Law

American Law and Economics Association (ALEA)
P.O. Box 208245
New Haven, CT 06520-8245
http://www.law.yale.edu/alea/

Marketing and Sales

For information about careers in sales and marketing management, contact

American Marketing Association
250 S. Wacker Dr.
Chicago, IL 60606

Promotion Marketing Association of America, Inc.
322 8th Ave., Ste. 1201
New York, NY 10001

Sales and Marketing Executives International
458 Statler Office Tower
Cleveland, OH 44115

Market Research

Council of American Survey Research Organizations
3 Upper Devon
Port Jefferson, NY 11777

Marketing Research Association
2189 Silas Deane Hwy., Ste. 5
Rocky Hill, CT 06067

Public Relations

Information about careers in public relations management is available from

Public Relations Society of America
33 Irving Pl.
New York, NY 10003-2376

Real Estate

American Real Estate and Urban Economics Association (AREUEA)
Indiana University, Kelley School of Business
1309 East Tenth St., Ste. 738
Bloomington, IN 47405
http://www.areuea.org/

Science

Economic Science Association (ESA)
Professor R. Mark Isaac
Treasurer, Economic Science Association
Dept. of Economics
401 McClelland Hall
University of Arizona
Tucson, AZ 85721-0108
http://www.econlab.arizona.edu/esa/

ON-LINE RESOURCES

Business Job Finder: Explore Business Careers
http://www.cob.ohio-state.edu/dept/fin/osujobs.htm

Career Find-O-Rama
http://www.review.com/careers/find/car_search_form.html

Careers in Economics
http://www.sju.edu/~nfox/careers.htm

Chronicle of Higher Education
http://chronicle.merit.edu/

Economic Resources Online
http://www.yardeni.com/othereco.html#R10

Economics and Teaching
http://www.ikt.anadolu.edu.tr/econet/teachin.html

Economics Job Search
http://www.inomics.com/query/job_search

Finance Careers & Links
http://www.uncwil.edu/stuaff/career/finance.htm

Links to Internet Resources in Business and Economics
http://www.bschool.ukans.edu/intbuslib/virtual.htm

MegaLinks: Economics
http://www.clearinghouse.net/cgi-bin/chadmin/viewcat/
Business-Employment/economics?kywd++

Resources for Economists on the Internet
http://econwpa.wustl.edu/EconFAQ/EconFAQ.html

INDEX